Five-a-Day Plus One

The Vitamin B$_{12}$ Cookbook

To all those who give their time and energy
to help others at the Pernicious Anaemia Society

Five-a-Day Plus One

The Vitamin B$_{12}$ Cookbook

A Collection of Recipes to Combat
a Common Dietary Deficiency

Martyn Hooper MBE

With a Foreword by
Patrick Holford

Hammersmith Health Books
London, UK

First published in 2020 by Hammersmith Health Books –
an imprint of Hammersmith Books Limited
4/4A Bloomsbury Square, London WC1A 2RP, UK
www.hammersmithbooks.co.uk

British Library Cataloguing in Publication Data:
A CIP record of this book is available from the British Library.

Print ISBN 978-1-78161-174-6
Ebook ISBN 978-1-78161-175-3

Commissioning editor: Georgina Bentliff
Cover designed by: Katy Simister and Madeline Meckiffe
Interior designed by: Madeline Meckiffe
Typeset and layout by: Katy Simister and Madeline Meckiffe
Index: Hammersmith Books Ltd
Production: Helen Whitehorn, Path Projects Ltd
Printed and bound by: Ashford Colour Press, Hampshire, UK
Pictures supplied by Shutterstock, the Pembrokeshire Beach Food Company
and Selwyn Seaweed Co, with permission

Contents

About the author

Martyn Hooper founded the Pernicious Anaemia Society when he was forced to take early retirement from teaching in further and higher education. The original purpose of the Society was to provide newly diagnosed patients with a 'plain English' explanation of their condition. The original online forum soon began to show that there were serious problems with the diagnosis and treatment of the disease, which causes vitamin B_{12} deficiency. Today, the Society has around 9,000 members from all over the world and, spearheaded by Martyn, campaigns to improve the diagnosis and treatment of pernicious anaemia.

Martyn was made an MBE in the Queen's New Year Honours List in 2016 for his work for sufferers of pernicious anaemia.

His previous books are:

Pernicious Anaemia: The Forgotten Disease
Living with Pernicious Anaemia and Vitamin B_{12} Deficiency
What You Need to Know About Pernicious Anaemia and Vitamin B_{12} Deficiency

Acknowledgements

My thanks go to Karyl Carter for loaning me her collection of old recipes; Fran, a real mermaid who works for the Pembrokeshire Beach Food Co, for allowing the reproduction of recipes and pictures; Katy Simister for introducing me to the world of design, and for researching, selecting and laying out most of the photographs in this book; and to my wife for once again having her home invaded by research books – in this case, cookery books.

Foreword

There are many myths about what constitutes a healthy diet and one of the biggest is that 'if you eat a well-balanced diet you will get all the nutrients you need'. Many people think they eat a 'well-balanced diet', but don't, and consequently – believing they get 'all the nutrients they need' – end up short in one or more essential vitamins. A classic example of such a deficiency is vitamin D – it is only very recently that we were all advised to supplement it in the darker winter months since it's made in the skin in the presence of sunlight.

Complacency about vitamin B_{12} is another classic problem. A great many people – perhaps one in four – do not eat enough food containing B_{12}, so don't absorb sufficient into their bloodstream to benefit from this vitamin's vital functions, which include keeping the brain and nerves healthy. A lack of B_{12} is one of the major drivers for Alzheimer's disease later in life. It is also an incredibly common cause of feeling tired all the time. This could be due to diet – for example, being largely vegan or vegetarian and not supplementing or eating foods fortified with B_{12} – or to decreasing absorption with age, exacerbated by common 'PPI' antacid medications[1] and, to a lesser extent, the diabetes drug metformin; or to an undiagnosed condition, pernicious anaemia, where the ability to absorb B_{12} is seriously compromised. To put this into context, for a combination of these reasons, one in three people over the age of 61 have insufficient B_{12} blood levels[2]. For these reasons, especially in older people, even the 2.5 mcg recommended daily allowance (RDA) is unlikely to be enough. However, the need for B_{12} is of paramount importance at every age. Pregnant women without it cannot make babies with healthy brains. Infants and children without it can't make the connections in their rapidly wiring brains that hardwire their intelligence. That is why this book is for everyone – young and old.

For this reason, I really like the '5 + 1 diet' idea. As great as veg and fruit and eating a more plant-based diet are, no plant gives a sufficient or reliable source of vitamin B_{12}. That's why you have to eat the '+ 1' of the title – something from eggs, dairy, seafood or animal origin. If you are vegan, the only reliable option is to supplement B_{12}, just as we all need to do with vitamin D in the winter. Fortunately, the foods high in B_{12} are also good for vitamin D, so following the '+ 1' guidelines in this book will make two big steps towards optimum nutrition.

No-one has worked harder to bring awareness of the vital importance of B_{12} in our diet, and in medicine, than Martyn Hooper and his wonderful team at the Pernicious Anaemia Society. This book translates their critical message about B_{12} into an easy understanding of the kinds of foods, meals and menus we need to ensure we have enough of this essential vitamin, with some simple and delicious recipes to boot. That's what we need – a 'B_{12}-eye's view' of our diet to know what a 'well-balanced diet' actually means in this regard. That is what *five-a-day plus one* does, and is why this guideline needs to be taught to us all, starting in schools. Read it, digest it and put it into practice in your daily life. Your health depends upon it.

Patrick Holford

Founder of the Institute for Optimum Nutrition

'There is no such thing as bad food;
just food and good food.'

Annie Gertrude Nora Hooper nee Gardener

(My late grandmother)

Introduction

I was on holiday in beautiful west Wales. I started out on a circular walk that would take me around four hours to complete. After about an hour the clouds began to gather and half-way through my walk the wind started to blow from the west and the drizzle that was falling soon turned into heavy and persistent rain. I was doing my best to convince myself that, even though the weather had turned foul, the views over the surrounding countryside and sea were still spectacular, but soon I was enveloped in a thick mist that meant the views had disappeared. When I passed a 'family-friendly pub' my natural instinct to shelter from the tempest got the better of me and I went inside. I was sitting near a window (I was on my own – I'm often to be found on my own) when a family of five appeared and sat on the table next to me. As they took off their waterproof jackets little pools of Welsh rain formed on the hard floor. I think that they had probably had enough of each other's company because they started to talk to me. The conversation was around the 'atrocious weather for August' theme. They started to read the family-friendly menu and ordered food. Now, I can't remember how this came about, but we started to talk about food, diet and healthy eating.

'My children know all about healthy eating,' the mother told me, and, to emphasise the point asked the youngest child, a pretty young girl of around 8 years whose hair and clothing were still making little pools of water on the floor, to tell me what 'healthy eating' was. 'It's five-a-day,' she told me, before returning her attention to the little puddles that were still forming around their table.

Now, here's a challenge – ask members of your family and friends what they understand to be a 'healthy diet' and the chances are that, if you live in one of the countries that have adopted a campaign to get people to eat more fruit and vegetables, you will be told that five-a-day is what we all should be aiming for. Even if they tell you that a healthy diet is a 'balanced' one, they will probably mention five-a-day as part of their answer. And this is testament to how successful the worldwide campaign has been that was started by the World Health Organization (WHO) to get us all to eat five portions of fruit and vegetables each day.

Why five-a-day?

During the 1980s, WHO had become aware that there was an alarming increase in heart disease and, following a number of research projects, it was found that people who ate around seven portions of fruit and vegetables per day – that's over 600 grams – suffered fewer heart-related deaths. So, they began a campaign to get people to include seven portions of fruit and vegetables per day in their diet. They also realised that getting people to eat seven portions was perhaps over-optimistic and so, in the early 1990s, WHO issued a guideline that the population should aim for at least 400 grams per day – that is, a more realistic target of five-a day.

In March 2003, the United Kingdom's government launched its five-a-day campaign to encourage people to eat at least five portions of fruit and vegetables per day – that's five portions in total, not five portions of fruit and another five of vegetables. This campaign was based on the guidelines from WHO, issued a decade earlier. Other countries introduced similar projects, with comparable catchy phrases.

Australia has '*Go for 2 & 5*' – that is, two fruit and five vegetables which means they fulfil the original WHO recommendation of seven portions a day. Canada has '*Fruits and Veggies – mix it up!*' – this is without a firm numerical recommendation. Germany's '*5 am tag*' goes for the magical five portions; New Zealand has an intriguing '*5 + a day*' campaign – does that mean six-a-day? Norway goes one better by including berries in their '*Fem om dagen*' (five a day). The United States promotes their '*Fruits and Veggies – More Matters*' – again, with no numerical indicator.

What counts as five-a-day?

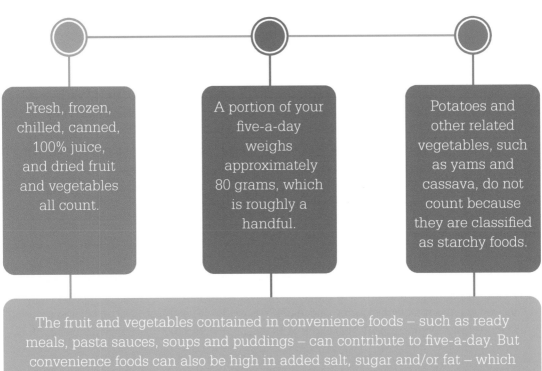

Fresh, frozen, chilled, canned, 100% juice, and dried fruit and vegetables all count.

A portion of your five-a-day weighs approximately 80 grams, which is roughly a handful.

Potatoes and other related vegetables, such as yams and cassava, do not count because they are classified as starchy foods.

The fruit and vegetables contained in convenience foods – such as ready meals, pasta sauces, soups and puddings – can contribute to five-a-day. But convenience foods can also be high in added salt, sugar and/or fat – which should only be eaten in moderation – so it's important always to check the nutrition information on food.

There are no reliable data to show just how successful the five-a-day programme has been. Commentators have pointed out that any improvement in health could be attributed to other measures taken by governments and individuals to improve the health of the general population, including the campaign to reduce the intake of salt and sugar, and encouraging people to take regular exercise. And there is also the problem of exactly what constitutes a portion – consider the difference in sizes of various apples. Along with this is the fact that some portions of fruit are very high in sugar – fruit juices in particular. Meanwhile, in 2004, a report by University College London stated that five-a-day was nowhere near enough fruit and veg; to have any benefits we should be eating 10-a-day.

Despite that, the five-a-day programme has become part of everyday language and, even if the recommendations are not followed rigorously, it can't be said that it hasn't made people aware of the need to include fruit and vegetables as part of their everyday diet; the little girl dripping onto the floor of the pub stands as testament to that.

There is a danger, however, of the five-a-day campaign being too successful in that people will believe that eating five portions of fruit and vegetables a day will, in itself, constitute a healthy and balanced diet. The fact is it doesn't, because no matter how much fruit or how many vegetables you eat, you will not be able to access one of the essential vitamins for good health – the amazing vitamin B_{12}, otherwise known as cobalamin.

The excellent website of the British Nutrition Foundation (BNF) www.nutrition.org.uk/healthyliving/ find-your-balance/portionwise.html is very useful in helping people like me understand what a balanced diet is, and they state that we should be eating:

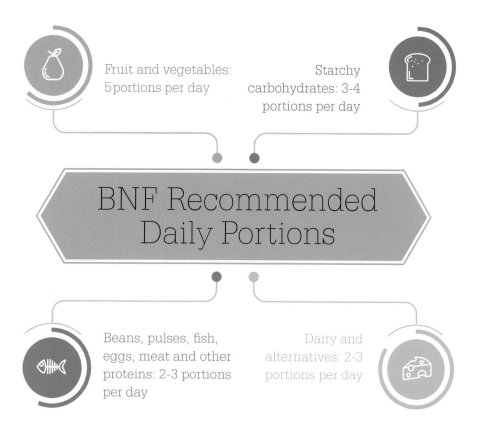

Fruit and vegetables: 5 portions per day

Starchy carbohydrates: 3-4 portions per day

BNF Recommended Daily Portions

Beans, pulses, fish, eggs, meat and other proteins: 2-3 portions per day

Dairy and alternatives: 2-3 portions per day

Ah! You see? A healthy diet is far from eating just fiveplus portions of fruit and vegetables (or seven or ten). And this is important because there is a serious worldwide problem of deficiency in one particular vitamin that is essential for good health - the aforementioned amazing vitamin B_{12}. That is what this book seeks to address.

The worldwide problem of vitamin B$_{12}$ deficiency

For my book *What You Need to Know about Pernicious Anaemia and Vitamin B$_{12}$ Deficiency* I crunched some numbers from the World Health Organization (WHO) and statistics from recent census reports and found that there is a worldwide problem with vitamin B$_{12}$ deficiency. In the West, about 10% of the population are too low in it. And no matter how many portions of fruit and vegetables you eat you will not absorb any vitamin B$_{12}$ from any of them. Vitamin B$_{12}$ is vital for good health, yet very few people are aware of its sources or the consequences of any deficiency. So, before we delve into the delicious B$_{12}$-rich recipes in this book, let's take a little time to get to know more about B$_{12}$

The vitamin B$_{12}$ molecule is the most complex of all vitamins.

Introducing vitamin B_{12}

What this book is about

This book goes some way to addressing the worldwide problem of vitamin B_{12} deficiency. As I've said, the numbers I crunched for my last book led me to the astonishing conclusion that around 10% of the population in the developed world are deficient in the vitamin. As different countries have different eating habits, and different proportions of young and old, it's impossible to know the exact statistics for deficiencies but it is now generally agreed (as I found in my calculations) that around 10% of the population in the developed world who are deficient in B_{12}. What this book aims to do is to redress that problem by providing you with a wide range of recipes that are rich in vitamin B_{12} and thereby feed yourself, and maybe your family, in such a way that you will not become one of those deficient 10%.

What does vitamin B_{12} do?

I'll try to keep this simple; if you need a more detailed explanation you could turn to the remarkable *What You Need to Know about Pernicious Anaemia and Vitamin B_{12} Deficiency* by a chap called Martyn Hooper (available on Amazon and in all good bookshops).

Basically, vitamin B_{12} is needed to form healthy red blood cells along with two other essential components – folate (vitamin B_9 or 'folic acid'), and iron. Without B_{12} the red blood cells become a funny shape and, because they are not the usual healthy shape, they cannot then carry oxygen to wherever it is needed in the body – which happens to be everywhere. Without oxygen being able to do what it should be doing the patient who is deficient in B_{12} will start to experience the symptoms of B_{12} deficiency – that bit's covered below (page 12), so keep reading. Vitamin B_{12} is also important in forming the myelin sheath that coats all nerve cells and nerve fibres, so without adequate levels of B_{12}, nerve damage can occur – often serious nerve damage that cannot be rectified; this I know because for several years I was deficient – seriously deficient - in vitamin B_{12} and I've got permanent damage to my central and peripheral nervous systems because of that deficiency. I experienced first-hand just how being deficient in this often-overlooked vitamin can affect everyday life. I was transformed from being an honest, decent, virtuous human being into a monster to live with and to be taught by. (I was working as a college lecturer at the time.) I was short-tempered, experienced sudden mood-swings, couldn't remember anything, talked gibberish at times and sought silence and solitude (not ideal when you are a busy lecturer in further and higher education). And though some of the symptoms have subsided, I still, like many people whose deficiency has been corrected, continue to experience the worst consequences of being B_{12}-deficient. Believe me, as someone who has lived with a vitamin B_{12} deficiency, you really don't want to go there – so make sure your diet contains sources of this extremely important and often overlooked vitamin.

As well as being essential for healthy red blood cells and a properly functioning nervous system vitamin B_{12} also plays an important part in maintaining a healthy immune system which is needed to fight diseases such as the recent Covid-19 virus. Here's what researchers Mikkelsen and Apostolopoulos say:

> *A substantial proportion of the global population does not meet the recommended daily intake of nutrients. Chronic diseases can arise from even marginal deficiencies. A change in regulation of the immune system can arise from insufficient intake of micronutrients. In particular, there*

is evidence that folic acid (vitamin B$_9$) and cobalamin (vitamin B$_{12}$) play a crucial role in the healthy balance of the immune system. Inadequate levels of folic acid and B$_{12}$ can drastically alter immune responses by affecting the production of nucleic acid, protein synthesis, inhibiting the activity of immune cells, and interfering with metabolic processes, including methylation and serine, glycine, and purine cycles. Inefficient methylation can lead to hyperhomocysteinemia which causes systemic and vascular inflammation contributing to the pathogenesis of many other diseases' [3]

You should, by now, be starting to appreciate just how wonderful and amazing vitamin B$_{12}$ is and how important it is that you include it as part of your everyday diet. Now we'll take a look at what foods contain it.

Sources of vitamin B$_{12}$

With very few exceptions, vitamin B$_{12}$ is found only in animal products – meat, fish and dairy. It is found in different concentrations. For example, 100 grams (g) of grilled back bacon will contain 1 microgram (mcg) of B$_{12}$ whereas 100 g of reduced-fat liver paté gets you 12 mcg. Some foods, notably some breakfast cereals, are *fortified* – they have vitamin B$_{12}$ added to them to compensate for there being no B$_{12}$ in the grains used.

However, there's also the strange matter of 'bio-availability' of the B_{12} in different foods – that is, how much that is there can we humans actually make use of. Dairy products contain fair amounts of B_{12} as does fish, but dairy products 'give up' their B_{12} more easily than meat or fish do; so the vitamin B_{12} in dairy products is more bio-available.

Meat, fish and dairy products are all good sources of B_{12}, but the two big players are offal and shellfish. Compared with rump steak, which has 3 micrograms per 100 grams, lamb kidneys have 54 micrograms per 100 grams, while cockles have 47 micrograms per 100 grams. This means that you really wouldn't have to eat much offal or shellfish to get your 2.4 microgram recommended daily intake of B_{12}.

As I have said, some other foods, such as breakfast cereals and yeast extracts, including Marmite and Vegemite (see below), have B_{12} added to them – they are 'fortified' with B_{12}. And, of course, you can buy vitamin B_{12} as an oral supplement which means you can live on vegetables and fruit as long as you remember to take a daily supplement of B_{12} as well.

However, be aware that there is some controversy over the type of B_{12} found in supplements. The controversy centres around 'analogues' of B_{12}. Analogues are variants of B_{12} in that their chemical structure differs slightly from 'true' B_{12}. I'll leave it at that because scientific debate about this issue has only recently started. I will say that of all the vitamins, B_{12} has the most complex chemical structure, earning Dorothy Crowfoot Hodgkin, who described it, the Nobel Prize in Chemistry in 1964.

Non-animal sources of B_{12}

As well as supplements, B_{12} can be found in some foods other than animal products, but there are differences of opinion as to the actual B_{12} content of these foods and the bioavailablity of the vitamin in them. For example, one reputable source states that shiitake mushrooms have a zero B_{12} content whilst other sources claim that 100 g of dried shiitake mushrooms provides 5.6 g.[4]

An alternative source states that: 'High levels of vitamin B_{12} were detected in the commercially available dried shiitake mushroom fruiting bodies (*Lentinula edodes*), which are used in various vegetarian dishes. The vitamin B_{12} contents of dried shiitake mushroom fruiting bodies (100 g dry weight) significantly varied and the average vitamin B_{12} value was approximately 5.61 mcg.'[5]

Another plant source of B_{12} is seaweed, especially dried nori used in sushi dishes: 'Dried nori sheet products… contain substantial amounts of B_{12} (approximately 77.6 µg/100 g dry weight)'. And: 'Our results and unpublished data have indicated that dried Chinese nori (zicai), dried New Zealand nori (karengo), dried Korean nori (kim), and canned Welsh nori (laverbread) contain approximately 60.2, 28.5, 66.8, and 2.8 µg of B_{12} per 100 g weight, respectively'.[6]

I have included some recipes with laverbread but have steered clear of any recipes involving raw fish.

Yeast extract

As I mentioned above, yeast extracts, such as Marmite and Vegemite, are generally fortified with B_{12}. I remember that in my primary school there were posters encouraging us to eat a healthy diet and yeast extract figured prominently on these posters. We were encouraged to eat a portion of the lovely salty, sticky, black stuff every day, and, of course, many millions of people do spread it on their toast every morning. However, what if you or any of your family members don't like the taste? Easy – add it to other foods. Simply add a teaspoon or so to stews, soups and gravy. While B_{12} does not occur naturally in the spread, being fortified makes it an excellent source of B_{12} for vegans and vegetarians.

How B_{12} is absorbed

The magical process of absorbing B_{12} from food involves some very complicated biochemistry, but I'll try to keep this as simple as possible; it's important to know the basic principles involved as this will allow you to understand the many ways B_{12} absorption can go wrong. It begins with special cells called parietal cells that line the wall of the stomach and excrete hydrochloric acid, which we need to break down protein, and an essential substance called intrinsic factor (IF). Intrinsic factor is a protein that binds to the B_{12} in any animal product you have eaten and allows it to be absorbed; without IF the B_{12} cannot be used. This absorption then takes place in the final section of the small intestine – the ileum. The B_{12} can then be sent off into the bloodstream where, along with iron and folate, it helps produce healthy red blood cells.

Causes of vitamin B_{12} deficiency

As I have said, vitamin B_{12} deficiency is a worldwide problem and there are many causes of this, including:

Vegetarianism and veganism: Vitamin B_{12} is found almost exclusively in animal products such as fish, meat and dairy, so, obviously one group of people who are at risk of developing a deficiency are vegetarians and vegans. Vegetarians who eliminate fish, meat and seafood from their diet but eat dairy products and eggs will probably be able to get enough B_{12} from their diet because, as mentioned above, the vitamin is more bio-available in dairy. Vegans who don't eat any animal products at all are at risk of developing a deficiency, though most will recognise this and take an oral supplement. As described, there are some non-animal sources of B_{12} but there is controversy as to how much B_{12} there is in these sources and how bio-available they are.

Modern medicines: Some medicines interfere with the metabolism of B_{12} in one way or another. These include the contraceptive Pill, metformin (used to treat type 2 diabetes), colchicine (for gout), cimetidine and other histamine H2 blockers (for peptic ulcers), omeprazole and lansoprazole (for acid reflux) and phenobarbital, pregabalin, primidone and topiramate (anti-epileptics). The impact of these drugs on the patient's vitamin B_{12} will vary, but all of the above will have some effect and lower levels. However, there is no acknowledged consensus of just how much patients' B_{12} levels are affected, but, if you are taking any of the above you may want to consider taking additional B_{12} supplements, perhaps after discussing this with your doctor.

Gastric bypass surgery and ileostomy: Vitamin B_{12} is absorbed in the ileum, which is the last part of the small intestine; this means that surgically removing the ileum (ileostomy) will render the patient unable to absorb B_{12} from food ever again. Meanwhile, gastric bypass surgery can involve reducing the stomach by as much as 90% which will compromise the production of IF and greatly reduce the amount available. So, those who have had an ileostomy or have undergone gastric bypass surgery will need to have injections of vitamin B_{12} for life because they won't be able to absorb B_{12} from either food or oral tablets.

Nitrous oxide (N_2O, 'laughing gas'): This is the UK's most popular recreational drug after alcohol and cannabis. It is widely available in clubs and at music festivals, where it is sold in balloons. (It is also used in dental surgery and as 'gas and air' during childbirth.) Just how nitrous oxide depletes the user's B_{12} involves quite complex biochemistry but essentially the N_2O splits into free nitrogen and free oxygen that quickly inactivates the B_{12}. And that's as far as I can go on that.

Gastric atrophy: This is due to chronic inflammation of the stomach lining leading to the parietal cells that produce IF and hydrochloric acid being replaced by fibrous tissue. This inflammation can be caused by infection, e.g. by the bacterium *Helicobacter pylori*, or by autoimmune attack; it is also associated with ageing. Whatever the cause, it will mean that the person will no longer be able to produce enough IF and consequently won't be able to absorb as much B_{12} from food as formerly.

Parasites: A number of parasites can reduce the functioning of the gut, including the fish tapeworm (*Diphyllobothrium latum*) which can be caught from eating raw fish, and the parasite *Giardia lamblia* that causes giardiasis, sometimes known as 'beaver fever'.

Pernicious anaemia: Ah! This is what I have. For some unknown reason I produce an antibody that neutralises the IF that I produce; I produce intrinsic factor antibodies. It is likely that this is the most common cause of vitamin B_{12} deficiency but it's notoriously difficult to diagnose because the test for the antibody is only around 50% reliable. (I tested negative for the antibody twice before testing positive.)

Tests for B$_{12}$ status

As we're on the subject of tests, or 'assays', you might as well also be aware that the test used to evaluate the B$_{12}$ status of patients is next to useless; there are two reasons for this.

1.   Active v. inactive B$_{12}$: Firstly, the current test used to determine a person's B$_{12}$ status – the serum B$_{12}$ test – measures the total amount of B$_{12}$ in the blood and doesn't differentiate between the biologically 'active' form of B$_{12}$ (called holo-transcobalamin) and the biologically 'inactive' B$_{12}$ (holo-haptocorrin). Now I could spend a lot of time here attempting to explain the extremely complex biochemistry behind all of this, but I would struggle to do so and there's the very real chance that I'd just confuse myself and, more importantly you. So, let's leave it at this – up to 90% of your total B$_{12}$ *can* be the 'inactive' type. I'm not saying that 90% of your circulating B$_{12}$ *is* inactive; I'm saying 'up to' 90% can be, which means that between 0 and 90% of your B$_{12}$ may be 'inactive' and the current blood test used to evaluate your B$_{12}$ status will not tell you about this. There are other markers that can be used to assess the status of B$_{12}$ in people, such as measuring methylmalonic acid and homocysteine levels along with the 'active' B$_{12}$ test, but these are not commonly done.

2.   No consensus on the parameters for deficiency: The second reason why the serum B$_{12}$ test is an unreliable indicator of a person's B$_{12}$ status is that there is no real consensus on what figure constitutes a deficiency let alone a sub-clinical deficiency (too low without any obvious symptoms); this means that some clinicians might consider a certain numerical value as being normal whilst another would consider it low. New guidelines[6] tell doctors that if the test shows 'normal' B$_{12}$ status but the patient has the symptoms of a deficiency, then the test result should be ignored and the patient treated with injections of B$_{12}$ to prevent any nerve damage – more of that on the next page.

Important note: If you have pernicious anaemia none of the recipes in this book will be of any use to you as you simply won't be able to absorb any B$_{12}$ from the foods. (This will also be the case if you have had an ileostomy.) Having said that, from the mid 1920s until after the Second World War the only treatment for pernicious anaemia was to feed the patient raw, or lightly cooked, liver in the hope that some B$_{12}$ would be 'passively absorbed'. I have been unable to source any data as to how successful this treatment was, but presumably it wasn't that successful – or easy to follow – or there would have been no need to develop B$_{12}$ injections; these injections mean that people can be treated and kept alive, though a great many will still experience the symptoms of the disease to some extent or other – there is still no cure for pernicious anaemia.

(As an historical aside, the use of liver and other offal to keep patients with pernicious anaemia alive was stumbled upon by accident, and nobody at the time knew that it was vitamin B$_{12}$ in the liver that was increasing the survival chances of the patients; indeed, they didn't know of any such vitamin as it wasn't discovered, or rather identified, until the late 1940s. Because shellfish, such as cockles, are exceedingly rich in B$_{12}$ the hapless patients might have benefited just as much from eating seafood – but the doctors at the time simply didn't know this. See Appendix 2 for examples. of the daily diet that patients with pernicious anaemia were fed to (hopefully) keep them alive in those pre-injection times.)

Symptoms of B₁₂ deficiency

There are two major problems with the symptoms associated with vitamin B_{12} deficiency. Firstly, they are insidious, which means they appear gradually and over many years, and what starts off as a mild irritant that can be easily ignored will, over time, significantly impact everyday life. Secondly, they are often associated either with getting older or with other diseases and illnesses, and, because of these two issues – insidious onset and other apparent causes – any possible B_{12} deficiency is often overlooked, sometimes for many years, before being correctly identified. Along the way the patient may be misdiagnosed repeatedly.

The list of symptoms below is long and yet not complete. I make no apologies for its length, but please be aware that there is probably no part of the human body that is not affected by any B_{12} deficiency as all parts of the body need an adequate oxygen supply. Here we go:

- Tiredness – tired all the time (sometimes abbreviated by doctors as TATT – not something you want to see on your medical records), waking up tired even after a good night's sleep, sleepy in the afternoon.
- Lethargy, sluggishness, lassitude, exhaustion, constant fatigue.
- Brain fog, confusion, cognition problems, memory loss (short-term), nominal aphasia (word-retrieval problems, the inability to think of the right word for an everyday object).
- Sudden mood changes and irritability.
- Balance problems (ataxia), the 'shoulder bumps', unusual gait, dizziness.
- Numbness and/or pins and needles (particularly in the hands and feet).
- Psychosis, delusions.
- Blurred or double vision.
- Premature greying of hair, hair loss.
- Cracking at the corners of the mouth (angular cheilitis).
- Swollen or 'beefy' or cracked tongue.
- Mouth ulcers.
- Sudden unaccountable bouts of diarrhoea, floating stools.
- Loss of libido.
- Incontinence.
- Shortness of breath ('the sighs').
- Palpitations, irregular heartbeat.
- Sudden shooting pains (especially down one side of the body).
- 'Electric shocks' down the spine or when tilting the head forward
- ('Lhermitte's sign' also known as the 'barber chair phenomenon').
- Painful and tired legs…

There are more, but that's enough to be going on with. The fact is that, as I mentioned above, there is no one part of the body that is not affected by B_{12} deficiency. The message then is clear – make sure that you have an adequate intake of B_{12} in your diet especially if your ability to make use of what you consume is compromised.

This book contains a selection of recipes that contain decent amounts of dietary B_{12}. Some of the dishes contain exceptionally high amounts of the vitamin whilst others contain enough to ensure you get your daily requirement, which is discussed below.

How much B_{12} do I need?

The recommended amount is around 2.5 micrograms per day (micrograms is shortened to mcg or μg). I know – that's quite meaningless isn't it? Let's put it this way: you don't need much. Think of a paperclip, those no-nonsense ones without the pretty plastic coverings. That paperclip weighs about a gram (g). There are 1000 milligrams (mg) in a gram and 1000 micrograms (mcg) in a milligram; in other words 1 mcg is one millionth of a gram. So, and good luck with this if you do try it, if you were to straighten out the paperclip and, with a great amount of care, and with your glasses on, cut it into 1000 pieces you would have 1000 bits of paperclip each weighing 1 milligram. You may find it easier to do if you cut the paperclip in half first and then cut each half into 500 little pieces? However you do it, you will then need to take one of the little 1 mg pieces and cut that into another 1000 pieces and each one of those pieces would weigh a microgram. Now, take one of those 1-mcg pieces and cut it in half. If you take two of the 1-mcg pieces and one of the 0.5-mcg pieces, put them together either on top of each other or side by side, that's how much vitamin B_{12} you will need per day; unless you are pregnant when you'll need to cut the other half of the 1-mcg piece into five and add one of the slivers to give you 2.6 mcg. Add another sliver or two to give you 2.7 or 2.8 if you are breastfeeding.

Now, why am I telling you this? I'm trying to show you that you don't need much of this vitamin so essential to good health, and that actually trying to measure your intake would be very time consuming and could very well take over your life.

It's the same when trying to measure the intake of B_{12} in food. The vitamin B_{12} content of foods was first investigated by two of the giants of nutrition, Professor R A McCance, who was a medical doctor, and Dr Elsie Widdowson, one of the first women to graduate from Imperial College London and who went on to become a renowned dietitian. In 1940 they published their *Chemical Composition of Foods*. The seventh revised edition of their work was published in 2015 and delivers just what the title promises – the chemical composition of the foods that we eat, including their vitamin B_{12} content. It's a big book and it takes some time to get used to using it. Almost all foodstuffs known to us are analysed in terms of their mineral and vitamin content, and the numbers given relate to 100 grams of that particular food. You have to remember that different foods have different densities – 100 grams of a light foodstuff, such as salmon mousse, would fill a plate, while a single slice of liver would weigh the same.

All of the recipes in this book feature ingredients that have decent amounts of B_{12} in them; some will provide all of your daily intake, while others will form part of the recommended intake, but all contain some B_{12} and, remember, you don't need much.

Supplementary B$_{12}$

You may now be wondering why you shouldn't just forget about including sources of B$_{12}$ in your diet and rely on taking an oral supplement as a substitute. Yes, that would be one way of ensuring that you got your daily intake. In fact, an awful lot of you already take vitamin and mineral supplements. A report by Mintel in Sept. 2016 valued the UK's vitamin and mineral supplements market at £414 million in 2015, with a 2.2% rise over the previous year. And that growth was expected to carry on. Altogether 54% of respondents to a survey conducted by the Health Food Manufacturers Association in 2017 believed they didn't get all of their daily vitamin and mineral requirements from food, and 45% of people who take supplements take them five days a week or more. So how come B$_{12}$ deficiency is such a problem? It could be that many of the multivitamins don't contain any or enough of B$_{12}$ (multivitamins are the most widely used supplements). Then there's the issue of analogues of B$_{12}$ as we saw above. Or there may be other reasons that have yet to be identified. However, we are skirting around the central issue which is that if you and your family eat a balanced diet that includes sources of B$_{12}$, then supplementation might not be needed – remember that for thousands of years the human race managed to live without any supplements, though that doesn't mean that there were no vitamin or mineral deficiencies in the past. And anyway, eating food is not just a necessity – it's part of the human way of life. We eat with friends and family, we eat to celebrate special occasions, we eat as part of religious rituals and, at the end of the day, food, if properly prepared, is delicious. Have you ever been invited to a supplement party? No! Please don't say yes to that.

About the recipes

My original aim for this book was to compile a series of B$_{12}$–rich dishes that would give you an idea about how much each contained. However, after six months of calculations and hours of frustration I decided that being exact about this was almost impossible because people eat different sized portions. And you might only have to eat a few grams of one particular food to get your necessary daily intake of B$_{12}$ whilst others would require you to eat a hefty amount. Look, I'll come clean – I got myself terribly confused and so I thought I'd just compile a set of recipes that have B$_{12}$ in them.

The recipes I've included all contain at least one item that has a decent amount of B$_{12}$ in it, by which I mean it has more than 1 microgram per 100 grams in weight. This has meant that an egg fried in vegetable oil wouldn't make it as it contains 1 mcg per 100 g while a boiled egg would as it contains 2 mcg per 100 g. A medium-sized chicken egg weighs about 50 g by the way.

Nobody in preceding centuries measured how much B$_{12}$ was in foods, nor for that matter did they measure any other nutritional content. People ate as varied a diet as they could. It's easy to imagine the children of Stone-Age people being told by their mothers to 'eat your greens', though what those greens would have looked like is anybody's guess. In short, what I'm giving you here are dishes that all have good amounts of B$_{12}$ in them, but some more, in some cases much more, than others. What is important is that you include some B$_{12}$–containing food in your diet each day in order to achieve your five-a-day plus one – the plus one being some vitamin B$_{12}$.

I have included some forgotten recipes, not only because they are good sources of B$_{12}$ but also because they are tasty and generally very cheap to produce. I haven't included recipes that, although rich in B$_{12}$, are prohibitively expensive. Nor have I included many that are rich in B$_{12}$ but the home cook would find difficulty getting his or her family to eat. Examples of such highly nutritious dishes include boiled lambs' brains – 'like eating clouds' - conger eel, dried eggs, boiled chickens' giblets and stewed ox liver. If you do want to introduce your family or friends to these exceptional sources of B_{12}, please let me know the outcome.

I have collected these recipes from family, friends and old family recipe books. The photographs are stock photographs that give an idea of how the dish would look on the table. Be adventurous and deviate from the ingredients if you wish – adding more of your favourite ones and reducing the ones you are not so keen on while making sure not to jettison the key sources of B_{12} I have included.

Overdosing on B_{12}

You can't overdose on B_{12}. Any excess is stored in the liver and when that organ is saturated you just get rid of the excess in your urine. This is all looked after automatically by your body; you don't have to make a special effort to store the vitamin or excrete it.

Back to a balanced diet

As I have said, the recipes that I have included all contain decent amounts of vitamin B_{12} and most also contain other essential vitamins and minerals. However, it will be up to you to add additional ingredients to make a 'balanced diet' according to the dietitians' guidelines on page 3. I haven't taken into consideration either calorie count, fat content or any other aspect that goes into eating healthily. Remember, around 10% of the population of the UK is thought to be deficient in B_{12} and these recipes are intended to correct any deficiency from diet. B_{12} is an essential ingredient in any diet just as much as any other vitamins and minerals are.

Breakfast .....

'Never work before breakfast; if you have to work before breakfast, eat your breakfast first.'

Josh Billings (19th century American humourist, 1818 – 1885)

Breakfast-time affords the ideal opportunity to get your daily dose of B_{12} as traditional breakfast foods are often high in B_{12}. And in the UK we do breakfast big-time, or at least we used to. One prolific author was once heard to proclaim that to eat well in England you had to eat breakfast three times a day.

Breakfast, as a meal, has a strange history. In ancient times, 4000 years before the beginning of agriculture, people were grinding wild wheat into flour and adding water to it to make either bread or porridge.[9] However, 'breaking the fast' was not considered an important meal and in the Middle Ages was even considered to be a sin by Thomas Aquinas, who associated it with gluttony. Gradually it evolved so that by the 15th century left-over meat and fish were added to the bread, nuts and weak beer that were consumed as the first meal of the day.

Then the introduction of caffeine drinks during the 16th century gave rise to the belief that tea and coffee would lead to the 'evacuation of superfluities' which can only be a good thing – and if anyone should ask why you drink tea or coffee for breakfast you now have an answer for them: 'I'm evacuating my superfluities.'

By the 19th century, breakfast had more or less developed into what it is today in that it had become a regular mealtime. Obviously, what was on offer would depend on how much money a family had to spend on foodstuffs, but the staples were now there – eggs and pork in the form of bacon being firm favourites.

Breakfast cereals – a brief history

Breakfast cereals were developed in the second half of the 19th century in the United States, where they were introduced initially to the growing number of health resorts called 'sanatoriums' (or more correctly in the plural, 'sanatoria'). People who were concerned about their health attended these institutions and were fed a vegetarian diet, which was considered far healthier than a balanced diet, and were denied any alcohol, tobacco, tea or coffee. And the best bit is, they actually paid for the privilege of being denied these 'luxuries'! Why they didn't just stay at home, eat fruit and vegetables and cut out alcohol, tea and coffee, which would have cost nothing, I can't figure out unless, of course, they craved the company of others undergoing the same treatment; maybe they needed that moral support and encouragement.

Breakfast cereals were heavily promoted to the public, and competition was fierce. As their uptake as a quick and easy 'healthy' breakfast grew, promotional techniques included puzzles on the backs of packets and free toys, hidden among the increasingly sugary flakes. Cartoon characters were introduced (think elves and roaring tigers) and this, coupled with people leading busier lives and mothers no longer staying at home to look after the husband and children, meant that traditional cooked breakfasts, in whatever form, were gradually replaced by the more convenient cereal and milk.

To buck this trend, the British Egg Marketing Board launched their 'Go to Work on an Egg' campaign (the slogan was crafted by the then unknown novelist Fay Wheldon) during the 1950s and 60s in an attempt to recover some of their market share as a breakfast food. It was perhaps successful in slowing down the decline in the traditional breakfast staple, but it couldn't halt the rise of breakfast cereals that were helped by the 'freebies' to be found in their boxes.

Over the latter half of the 20th century, vitamins were added to the cereals to compensate for the loss of nutritional value during the manufacturing process: firstly vitamins B_9 (folate/folic acid) and D, and sometime later our friend B_{12}, along with thiamine (B_1), riboflavin (B_2), niacin (B_3), pantothenic acid (B_6) and iron. Most cereals, including the various brands of corn flakes and bran flakes, are currently fortified with B_{12} though it is still possible to buy unfortified examples, but you'll have to look hard. Wheat biscuits and shredded wheat-type cereals are generally not fortified with B_{12} though I have been unable to discover why.

Breakfast cereals with milk

Let's start off with a bowl of fortified bran flakes, corn flakes, malted wheat flakes or chocolate-flavoured crispy rice, all served with milk. All of these cereals are fortified with B_{12} – just look at the information on the packets. The amount of B_{12} stated is usually per 100 grams (g). Sometimes the producer will also state the amount per serving. But how big is a serving? Well, you know those little boxes of cereals that you get in budget hotels? They contain a single serving of between 20 and 40 g. (You may get those in expensive hotels as well, but I've never stayed in an expensive hotel.) Breakfast cereals can be eaten 'dry' but, like the vast majority of people, I prefer to add milk, which itself contains B_{12} as well: 9 micrograms (mcg) per 100 g. A litre of milk weighs just over 1000 g, so half a litre will give you around 5 mcg of B_{12} which is double your recommended intake.

Realistically, a bowl of cereal will be eaten with about a quarter of a litre so that alone will provide you with your recommended intake – assuming you have no problems with processing and absorbing it. And, to brighten up this page, here's a beautiful photograph of a bowl of highly nutritious (in terms of B_{12}) cereal with milk.

The continental breakfast

Not all societies have benefited from the joy of tucking into a 'full English', or the even more delicious 'full Welsh' breakfast (more of that later – page 29). Those on the continent of Europe still have their own way of ensuring that breakfast contains a decent hit of B_{12}, although it takes a bit of getting used to if you are not a native. Ham, cheese, eggs, salami and sausages all contain decent enough quantities of B_{12} to ensure that the diner's B_{12} intake gets off to a good start. The British interpretation of the 'continental breakfast' as a baguette with jam holds no such benefits.

Eggs

A boiled egg contains 2.0 mcg of B_{12} per 100 g (a typical medium-sized egg weighs around 40-50 g), so two eggs will get you 4 mcg which is on its way to being almost double your daily recommended intake. A scrambled egg in butter gets you your daily intake of 2.4 mcg; so, a couple of scrambled eggs on toast with butter will provide you with about double your recommended daily intake of B_{12}.

A single fried egg provides 1 mcg; egg yolk on its own, 6.9 mcg/100 g.

Scrambled eggs on toast

Serves 1

2 medium-sized eggs   **splash milk**
knob of butter

1   Crack the two eggs into a saucer and put to one side.

2   Put the knob of butter into a saucepan and begin to heat, then add the milk.

3   Heat until the butter has melted and then add the two eggs, stirring vigorously until they begin to 'set' or scramble.

4   Remove from the hob and let them continue to set in the residual heat.

5   To serve, tip the contents onto two pieces of buttered toast and add salt and black pepper to taste.

Serve with tomatoes and a sprinkling of your favourite herbs if you wish.

Cheese omelette

Serves 1

2-3 medium-sized eggs
knob of butter

pinch salt
handful grated cheddar cheese

1   Crack the eggs into a bowl and beat briskly until the mixture is smooth then add the salt.

2   Place the butter into a small frying pan and heat making sure the butter coats the bottom and sides of the pan by gently swirling the pan.

3   Add the egg mixture and, if you want to, add onions or herbs. Then, using a spatula, gently pull it in from the sides of the pan to the centre so that the mixture begins to set evenly.

4   It's probable that the mixture on the bottom of the pan sets before the top and so you can either place the pan under a hot grill for a few minutes or, invert the pan over a plate so that the undercooked mixture is on the bottom and then slide it back into the hot pan for a few more minutes. Serve with anything you fancy.

Seaweed

The strange case of seaweed

McCance and Widdowson (see reference 1 in on page 129) don't list the vitamin and mineral content of seaweed, which is surprising. Two particular types of seaweed – green dried laver (*Enteromorpha sp*) and purple laver (*Porphyra sp*) – contain significant amounts of B_{12}[11]. Nori, which is dried purple laver, is used extensively in Japanese sushi dishes and laverbread (which Richard Burton called the 'Welshman's caviar') is also made from purple laver; this seaweed contains 32.3 mcg per 100 g[3] which makes it a gold-standard food as far as vitamin B_{12} is concerned.

Laverbread (bara lawr in Welsh) is made from harvested laver seaweed, mainly from the West coast of Wales. After being thoroughly washed several times, the seaweed is boiled for at least six hours until it turns into a black mush. It is then fried on its own or after being rolled in oatmeal – see the next fabulous recipe from the Pembrokeshire Beach Food Company. In this case the 'Welshman's Caviar' refers to their own toasted seaweed relish that can be bought from their online store.

Welsh breakfast

I remember that when I was growing up my mother or father would reach into the fridge on a Sunday morning and retrieve laverbread and cockles to cook with the bacon and eggs that was the staple Sunday-morning breakfast. Both the laverbread and the cockles had been bought the night before from the 'cockle man'. The cockle man would carry a wicker basket full of seafood ingredients, including cockles, laverbread and crab-sticks, into every pub and club in the valley where I lived. People would buy what they needed and carry it home ready for breakfast the next morning. Crab-sticks would usually be eaten there and then – and if you haven't tried a pint of room-temperature bitter with a couple of crab-sticks then you really should.

Traditional Welsh breakfast with Welshman's Caviar

The Pembrokeshire Beach Food Company recommend using thick Pembrokeshire bacon, laverbread with oats, and a fried egg topped with Welshman's Caviar. To really celebrate the taste of Wales a handful of cockles cooked in Welsh Sea Black Butter can be added.

3 thick strips Welsh bacon
2 tbsp laverbread
2 tbsp oats

1 egg
1 tsp Welshman's Caviar
handful of cooked cockles (optional)

1   Heat a non-stick frying pan over a medium heat and then place your bacon in the pan

2   While the bacon is heating up, mix the laverbread and oats in a bowl and season with salt and white pepper to taste until they combine altogether

3   Once the bacon is sizzling away and the bacon fat starts releasing its juices, add the laverbread mix with a tablespoon and flatten gently into the frying pan until you get your desired thickness.

4   Continue cooking until bacon and laverbread cake are crispy, then add the egg and the Welshman's Caviar on top of the raw egg; gently cook until ready.

Serve with orange juice and tea.
Enjoy a lovely start to the day.

Devilled kidneys

Serves 2

This is a wonderful breakfast dish and well worth the effort to prepare. Devilled means 'hot' or 'peppery' and this dish was, and probably still is, a traditional country-house breakfast. Each kidney weighs around 30 g so two kidneys will get you around 750% of the recommended daily intake.

4 lambs' kidneys
2 tbsp plain flour
1-2 tsp curry powder
½ tsp English mustard powder
50 g butter
good glug olive oil
2 tsp tomato purée

1 clove garlic, peeled and crushed
50 ml chicken stock
1 tbsp double cream
salt
black pepper
2 slices toast

1   Remove the outer membrane from the kidneys and cut in half. Use a sharp pair of kitchen scissor to snip out the fatty core which can be very tough.

2   Put the flour, curry powder and mustard powder into a bowl and mix well. Toss the kidneys in the flour and then shake off any excess.

3   Melt the butter and oil in a frying pan and fry the kidneys until a golden colour.

4   Add the stock, double cream, tomato purée and garlic. Season to taste and cook for a further 2-3 minutes.

5   Serve on toast, adding a sprinkling of cayenne pepper if you want to be really Devilly!

Kippers

Kippers are herrings that have been 'butterflied' (split open), soaked in salt water and then smoked over oak chips. They can be fried, grilled, poached or jugged. Whichever way you cook them they will give you a good hit of B_{12} – 11 mcg/100 g if grilled, and even the boil-in-the-bag variety will get you 10 mcg/100 g.

Grilled kippers

Serves two

1   Cut the heads off the kippers if you wish.

2   Place the kippers onto a grill pan, skin-side up, and cover with half of the butter.

3   Grill under a medium to high heat for 5 minutes.

4   Carefully turn the kippers over and spread the remaining butter over them.

5   Grill for a further 5 minutes.

Often served with poached or scrambled eggs

Jugged kippers

1   Place the kippers in a large earthenware or heat-resistant glass jug.

2   Pour over boiling water and leave to stand for 10 minutes.

3   Drain and serve.

Poached kippers

1   Place the kippers in a large frying pan and cover with water.

2   Bring to the boil and simmer for 10 minutes.

3   Drain and serve.

Boil-in-the-bag kippers

These are convenient and quick and are an ideal way of ensuring a decent hit of B_{12}. Several brands are available and most of the supermarkets sell their own-brand versions. Simply follow the instructions on the pack.

No time for breakfast?

There are then, many ways to start the day with a good proportion of your daily B_{12} requirement. However, fewer of us apparently are eating breakfast. A report in the *Daily Express* from 2017 stated that around 50% of Brits skip breakfast and there is evidence that people who do eat breakfast have healthier lives[12]. Time, or lack of it, is probably why people don't eat breakfast, but preparing 'the most important meal of the day' needn't take more than a few minutes.

If you really are in a hurry here's my suggestion:

1   Pop two slices of bread into the toaster and leave them to brown whilst you are brushing your teeth.

2   Spread the toast thinly with butter and then with Marmite, or other vitamin B_{12}-fortified yeast extract;

Marmite has 24 mcg/100 g. (Incidentally, you know those little portions of Marmite you get in hotels and supermarket restaurants? They contain an 8 g serving of the spread which, if you like Marmite, is often not enough for one slice of toast and you end up using two per slice. Each 8 g serving gets you 1.9 mcg of B_{12} or 76% of your recommended intake. Two portions, spread on either one slice of toast or two, will get you 152% of your daily allowance, which means you can spend the rest of your day finding out exciting ways to eat your five-a-day. (Incidentally, if you want to smuggle out one or two of the portions from the hotel breakfast buffet, don't hide them in your trouser pocket because they get warm and can leak out. I know because it happened to me!)

If you are in a really big hurry, you can eat your toast spread with Marmite on your way to your car – but take care not to drop any on your clean shirt.

If you can't wait for the bread to toast, just use untoasted bread.

And if you haven't the time for that, you should really go to bed earlier or get a different job.

Chapter 2

Lunch .....

Lunch is the abbreviated form of 'luncheon', which is derived from the early Anglo-Saxon words *Nuncheon* or *Nunchin*, which means 'lunchtime drink'. In the Middle Ages, the main meal of the day took place after several hours' work and was called 'dinner', but in the 17th and 18th centuries 'dinner' was moved back to the early evening which meant there was a big gap between breakfast and dinner and 'luncheon' came to fill this.

There's a lot of confusion about the terms 'dinner' and 'lunch'. School children who take a packed lunch to school (in their lunch-box) will eat it at 'dinner time'. Pupils who eat food prepared by the school kitchen have 'school dinners'; and when I was growing up, you ate 'dinner' at lunch time, though we called it 'dinner time', and your late afternoon and main meal of the day was 'tea', which is what most working-class people did and still do.

Up until the early 19th century, lunch was usually eaten by women whose husbands were out at work (hence the phrase 'ladies who lunch') and usually involved left-overs from the dinner the night before. Mrs Beeton, writing in 1864, didn't have much to say about lunch compared with other meals.[13]

The remains of cold joints, nicely garnished, a few sweets, or a little hashed meat, poultry or game, are the usual articles placed on the table for luncheon, with bread and cheese, biscuits, butter, etc. If a substantial meal is desired, rump-steaks or mutton chops may be served, as also veal cutlets, kidneys... In families where there is a nursery, the mistress of the house often partakes of the meal with the children, and makes it her luncheon. In the summer, a few dishes of fresh fruit should be added to the luncheon, or, instead of this, a compote of fruit or fruit tart, or pudding.

Today, lunch can be a formal affair eaten at a restaurant, an informal 'pub lunch' or a hurried affair taken while still sitting at a desk in front of a computer. I'm going to concentrate on the people who don't have much time to eat their mid-day meal and so the ideas that follow are for quick and convenient foods that can be eaten when time is an issue but also contain decent amounts of B_{12}. If you have the time or budget to eat a more lavish and formal meal, simply choose a recipe from the 'Dinner' section of recipes (page 89).

Sandwiches

We begin with what for many is their chosen way to eat lunch. According to the *Wall Street Journal*, the sandwich is 'Britain's biggest contribution to gastronomy',[14] which is not just rude but shows an ignorance of real British food. Anyway, it was in the 18th century that John Montagu, the 4th Earl of Sandwich, supposedly asked his servant to fetch him some meat between slices of bread so that he could continue playing cards – the bread would have prevented the cards becoming greasy as would have happened if he had used his hands to hold the meat directly. However, Montagu's biographer, N A M Rodger, has suggested that, because of his work with the Royal Navy and in politics he is most likely to have ordered the first sandwich from his work-desk rather than the gaming table. Whatever the truth, it is said that others ordered 'the same as Sandwich' and one of the greatest culinary inventions was born.

There are several versions of sandwiches. However, I'm not convinced that an 'open sandwich' is really a sandwich at all; open sandwiches were first described by a 17th century naturalist when visiting the Netherlands where he observed that in the Dutch taverns meat hung from the ceilings and 'which they cut into thin slices and eat with bread and butter laying the slices upon the butter' – something which was obviously not done in the visitor's homeland of Great Britain. Then there's the issue of whether a bread roll with a filling can be classed as a sandwich, and that discussion could very well lead on to the rather sensitive matter of baps and butties. Ask yourself, is a bacon butty with brown sauce a sandwich? What would John Montagu make of it all?

Pre-packaged sandwiches

There is some debate as to when the first pre-packed sandwiches made their appearance in supermarkets. Whilst there were earlier attempts, it was Marks and Spencer who made a serious venture into mass sandwich selling in 1980 when five stores offered a limited range to the public. So successful was the pilot that it was rolled out to other stores and a year after they were first sold, Marks and Sparks were looking for companies who could mass-produce their growing range of sandwiches on an industrial scale. Now, pre-packed sandwiches are available not only from supermarkets but from smaller shops, filling stations, motorway services, newsagents – well, almost everywhere really. In 2017, the UK made and sold £8 billion-worth of sandwiches.

However, don't imagine that pre-packed sandwiches are a relatively new thing. For hundreds of years people were preparing sandwiches for families and friends to take with them wherever they were going. And these were tailor-made to the preference of the end-user where family income permitted; otherwise it was a basic staple of perhaps cheese and onions (some B_{12} there in the cheese) or leftover roast meat (again, some B_{12} there).

Whether you make your own concoction or buy ready-made sandwiches, there is an enormous variety of options for the hungry person. Below is a selection of sandwiches that are good sources of vitamin B_{12} – some more so than others. The list in Appendix I (page 119) gives the relative amounts in these foods but of course it depends how much of the B_{12}–rich ingredients you choose to use:

Making your own sandwiches

If you're going to make your own, can I suggest that you consider using a seafood cocktail filling for maximising B_{12}. This can be bought from most supermarkets, though I must warn you that whoever is opening their sandwich container should be sitting in a well-ventilated space!

Cheese and onion

Egg and cress

Liver paté

Prawn mayonnaise

Beef (and horseradish)

Salmon (on its own or with cucumber)

Chicken and sweetcorn

Tuna and sweetcorn

Otherwise, keep in mind that cheese and seafood are two excellent sources to consider putting in your sandwiches and all meat will have some B_{12}.

The wonders of pâté

How about a change from sandwiches? Try pâté on fresh crusty bread. Pâté is a paste made up of lean meat and fat which has been ground, sieved or puréed; patés can be coarse, medium or smooth depending on the level of processing.

Pâté baked in a crust or pie is known as *pâté en croûte*; if it's baked in a 'terrine' (deep dish) and wrapped in fat, then it's known as *pâté en terrine*. Most pâtés contain liver, which, as we know from the Introduction, is high in B_{12}. What is amazing about this superfood (in terms of B_{12}) is that there are so many variations. They range enormously in price (I've seen 100-gram packs for 40 pence in supermarkets), in ingredients and in taste, so they make a wonderfully varied source of dietary B_{12}.

My own particular favourite is smoked-mackerel pâté, which contains 18 mcg of B_{12} per 100 g, so a small serving of 25 g will give you almost double your daily recommended intake. Think about trying a ready-made verson when you are next browsing around the supermarket and wondering at the variety on offer. Or try making your own. Here's a really simple recipe; if you don't have a blender you can mash everything together with a fork

Smoked mackerel pâté

2 whole smoked mackerel
1 tsp grated horseradish
2 tbsp crème fraîche or cottage cheese
2 tsp Dijon mustard

pinch black pepper
juice of ½ lemon
100 g butter, chopped – salted or unsalted

1   Remove the skin from the fish and discard.

2   Place the fish in the blender and don't worry about the odd bone as everything is going to be blended.

3   Add the horseradish, crème fraîche, mustard, black pepper and lemon juice.

4   Blend until it becomes a rough paste, then add the butter and blend until smooth.

5   Season to taste with salt.

Serve on crusty white bread or sourdough bread.

Fast-food

Cheeseburgers

You could make your own cheeseburgers I suppose, but if the temptation of a quick and convenient take-away appeals, then you should know that a cheeseburger contains 2.0 mcg of B_{12}, which really does make it a valid part of a healthy balanced diet – just don't have the fries with it - there is no vitamin B_{12} in them.

Coated chicken breast

A stable-mate of the cheeseburger, 100 g of breadcrumb-coated chicken breast will provide you with more than your recommended daily intake – a full 3 mcg of B_{12}.

'Healthy' options

Be aware that many 'healthy' options available from sandwich bars, fast-food outlets and take-aways are *not* healthy in terms of B_{12} content. Veggie burgers, falafel and sprouted greens may have lots of health benefits going for them but absolutely no vitamin B_{12}.

Chapter 3

Soups .....

Vegetables, meat and liquid – together they make soup. The word 'soup' is derived from the French meaning 'broth'. This in turn is derived from the Latin for bread soaked in broth – *suppa*. A 'broth' is the liquid part of a soup and is my favourite word in the English language. Soups can be substantial meals in themselves, or they can be served as a starter or snack. They can be simple or intricate, but I'm just going to concentrate on soups that contain decent levels of B_{12} – so they will be animal or fish-based.

Seafood chowder

Serves four

8 medium potatoes
1 medium onion, diced
2 cloves of garlic
knob of butter
1 tbsp stock powder
1 tsp Captain Cat's Mor Seasoning

700 ml milk
200 g prawns
400 g fish (mix of white fish, pink fish
    and smoked fish)
100 ml cream

This soup recipe is from the Pembrokeshire Beach Food Company and is one of their best-sellers. The Captain Cat's Mor Seasoning can be bought from their website or you can use whatever spice blend you like.

1   Peel and chop up the potatoes, boil them in a pan until tender, then drain them and set aside.

2   Heat another pan and add the onion, garlic, butter, stock and seasoning. Cook for around 10 minutes over a gentle heat.

3   Meanwhile pour the milk into a saucepan and gently simmer over a low to moderate heat.

4   Add two thirds of the potatoes to the milk and then, with a hand-blender, puree the remaining third of the potatoes into a smooth paste.

5   Add the pureed potatoes to the milk and potato mixture - this will help to thicken the soup.

6   Now add the onion mix, prawns and fish.

7   Simmer until the fish and prawns are well cooked.

8   Remove from the heat and stir through the cream. Now it is ready to serve with crusty white bread.

Fish soup
Serves four

The good thing about fish soup is that you can use any fish and vegetables that are to hand. Here's a suggestion for ingredients but do adapt to match your preferences and available ingredients, so long as the amounts of fish and seafood are maintained.

2 small carrots
2 onions
2 celery stalks, all finely chopped
4 grated garlic cloves
small glass dry white wine
500 ml fish stock –- dissolve some fish stock cubes into boiling water
1½ litres vegetable stock –- use vegetable stock cubes
500 g carton or tin chopped tomatoes

8 fresh tomatoes, roughly chopped –- this gives added texture
2 anchovy fillets in oil
250 g cubed fish, making sure all the bones have been removed
250 g frozen seafood, defrosted and rinsed
salt and pepper
olive oil

1   You'll need a large, heavy-bottomed pan.

2   Heat the olive oil in the large pan and gently fry the carrots, onions, celery and garlic until soft but without any colour.

3   Add the dry white wine and simmer for around 5 minutes.

4   Add the fish and vegetable stock and the chopped tomatoes, then the fresh tomatoes and the anchovy fillets and a little black pepper.

5   Cover and simmer for about 40 minutes.

6   Add the cubed fish and defrosted seafood.

7   Cover and simmer for 20 minutes, stirring now and again.

Serve with crusty bread.

Haslet soup – Cawl Haslet

Serves three to four

This is a very unusual soup that is bound to become a talking point. The following recipe is from a very old Welsh, handwritten family recipe book. *Cawl* is the Welsh word for 'soup'.

500 g pigs' liver
500 g onions
2 l chicken stock

500 g potatoes
salt and pepper

1 Cut up the liver.

2 Peel and slice the onions.

3 Put the meat and onions into a large saucepan and pour over the stock.

4 Simmer for around 2 hours.

5 Peel the potatoes, cut into cubes and add to the pan.

6 Simmer for a further 30 minutes.

7 Add the salt and pepper.

8 Strain off the liquid and serve with a few sprigs of parsley and crusty white bread.

9 Discard the solids.

Korean seaweed soup with beef

(Soegogi miyeokguk or 쇠고기 미역국)*

Serves three to four

This is regarded as something of a super food in Korea where it is eaten as a special birthday treat. It is also traditionally given to new mothers soon after the birth as its nutritional content is believed to help the mother recover and produce breast milk. It's important to use any green or purple laver as these contain the 'active' form of B_{12} – wakame is ideal.

15 g dried wakame
120 g beef – any cut will do as long
  as you slice it into small pieces
pinch sea salt
pinch black pepper

1 tbsp sesame oil
1½ tbsp soy sauce
2 good pinches crushed garlic
1.25 l water

1 Start by soaking the seaweed in a large bowl of water for 10 minutes, by which time it will have expanded considerably. Rinse it for several minutes under running water, squeeze out the moisture and put it to one side.

2 In a bowl, season the beef pieces.

3 Heat the sesame oil in a large saucepan and add the beef and seaweed; fry for three minutes stirring all the time.

4 Add the soy sauce, garlic and water and give it a good stir.

5 Cover the pot and boil for about 15-20 minutes or until the meat is cooked.

Serve immediately.

NB: You can substitute any other protein for the beef; mussels are often used. For a vegan version, simply leave out the beef – it's still a delicious soup containing bioactive plant-based B_{12}.

Chapter 4

Snacks or light meals .....

The *Cambridge University Dictionary* defines a snack as 'a small amount of food that is eaten between meals, or a very small meal'. They are usually portable, made at home either from leftovers or from new ingredients. In recent years there has been a considerable increase in the number of processed snacks available which are often criticised for containing too much salt and sugar.

The recipes listed here are mainly light meals though I have included two highly portable items.

Sardines on toast

Serves two

This is one of the most popular snacks or supper dishes in the UK – and little wonder; it's devilishly easy to make. There are, however, two schools of thought on the best way to produce and serve the dish.

1 tin sardines (those in olive oil or sunflower oil have 15 mcg/100 g B_{12}; those in tomato sauce have 8 mcg/100 g)

4 slices bread
mayonnaise (optional)
splash lemon juice (optional)

1   Mash up the sardines in a bowl using a fork. If you want to go upmarket, add the mayonnaise and lemon juice at the start.

2   Make the toast.

3   Spread the sardines or sardine mixture onto the toast and enjoy.

Alternative method

1   Toast one side of the bread only (this is extremely difficult to do using a toaster – you'll have to use a grill)

2   Spread the sardines on the untoasted side and return to the grill so that the sardines are warmed through.

Serve immediately.

Cheese on toast

Serves one

All cheeses contain B$_{12}$, even the processed type. Cheddar cheese contains 2.4 mcg/100 g whilst fresh parmesan contains 3.3 mcg/100 g.

Here's another timeless classic that never fails to deliver. The cheese has to be thinly sliced; grated cheese tends to fall off the sides.

2 slices bread   thinly sliced cheese –- enough to
butter   cover the bread

1   Toast the bread and butter one side.

2   Cover the buttered side with the thinly sliced cheese, ensuring that none of the bread remains uncovered.

3   Pop it back under the grill, cheese side up.

4   Grill until the cheese is melted and bubbling.

5   Remove from the grill and serve, with Worcestershire sauce to taste.

Someone once remarked that cheese on toast is best enjoyed with a can of Stella Artois while watching football on the television. I can't comment as I don't like lager or football, but it might be worth giving it a go.

Parmesan toast

Serves four

Parmesan cheese contains more B_{12} than most other cheeses. This is a variation on the British classic cheese on toast, which can be eaten on its own, but it makes an excellent accompaniment for various soups.

8 thick slices of a baguette-type loaf
1 clove garlic, crushed
extra-virgin olive oil

about 120 g parmesan cheese, grated
coarse sea-salt
herbs of your choice (optional)

1   Heat the oven to 200°/fan 190°/gas mark 6.

2   Spread the garlic onto the bread slices and then drizzle with the olive oil

3   Cover each slice with the parmesan cheese and sprinkle with salt to taste.

4   Place the slices on a baking sheet in the oven and cook for around
     12 minutes or until they are browned to your liking.

Scrambled eggs with frankfurters

Serves one

This is one of my favourites – though I don't think many people will have tried it. Scrambled eggs with semi-skimmed milk contain 2.4 mcg/100 g and a frankfurter, or hotdog sausage, contains an additional 1 mcg/100 g. A standard-sized hotdog sausage weighs a very convenient 25 g.

2 medium eggs   salt
2-4 hotdog sausages –- standard size   black pepper
knob of butter   tomato ketchup (optional)
splash semi-skimmed milk

1   Heat the sausages in a pan of water.

2   Melt the butter in a frying pan.

3   Add a splash of milk.

4   Crack in the eggs.

5   Stir the eggs vigorously until they begin to set.

6   Turn off the heat and let the eggs continue to cook in the residual heat.

7   Drain the sausages and place on a warm plate.

8   Add the eggs.

9   Add salt and pepper to taste, and ketchup if wanted.

Liver sausage and crusty bread

Liver sausage is cheap and readily available from supermarkets or delicatessens. It is rich in B_{12} (10mcg/100 g).

Serve it spread on fresh, crusty bread for a simple, satisfying and nutritious snack.

Cockles

Now this has to be one of the ultimate convenience foods. Cockles can be bought loose in markets,… well in Wales at least. Wander around the wonderful indoor markets in Swansea or Cardiff and you'll see people picking at a polyester cup of cockles using a wooden fork if they are modernists, but traditionalists just use their fingers. Usually they are doused in vinegar and pepper.

They can also be bought as pickled cockles in jars in supermarkets. The drained weight of one of those jars is 155 g and they pack a considerable B_{12} punch – 47 mcg/100 g. So, finishing off a jar of cockles whilst sitting at your desk, or anywhere else, gets you over 90 mcg of B_{12} - that's around 3750% of your daily requirement.

Cockles and Magna Carta

Signed by King John in 1215, the Magna Carta has been associated with fairness, justice and human rights and, if you live in England or Wales, it gives you the right to collect up to 8 lb of cockles every year from the foreshore. To collect more than that, you need a licence..However, be careful if you want to exercise your right – always check tides and local conditions or, even better, go out with an experienced cockler. (Good luck with an internet search for that one!)

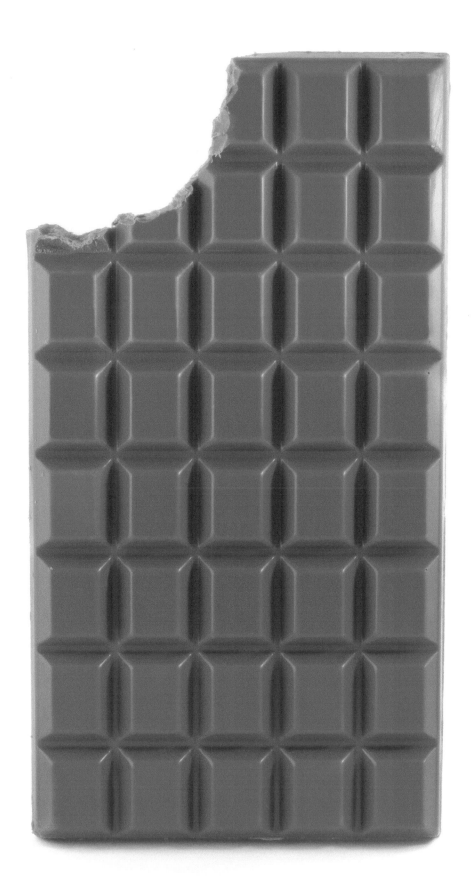

And also...

Tubed cheese

For topping up your B_{12}, this is a fantastic product that is found in all supermarkets, including discount stores. It's incredibly useful as a portable snack. I always used to carry a tube with me whenever I went hill-walking in the days before I developed nerve damage due to not being able to absorb B_{12}. When you feel peckish, simply squeeze the cheese into your mouth. (I have never done this without imagining that I'm an astronaut on the International Space Station because that's how they eat their meals!)

If you are not comfortable with eating it this way, you can always just squeeze some on crackers, but try the straight-in-the-mouth method first, even if you would prefer to do so without anyone watching.

Milk chocolate bar

And now for some good news. A 100 g bar of milk chocolate contains 2.1 mcg of B_{12} – nearly your full daily recommended intake. Plain chocolate contains no B_{12}.

One of those small 100 g boxes of Maltesers will provide you with just over half of your recommended intake – 1.3 mcg.

Seaweed thins

These are becoming more popular and are now widely available in supermarkets as well as health food shops and are a convenient way to give yourself a B_{12} boost. Dried nori has the highest concentration of B_{12} of all the seaweeds and is widely available in supermarkets and health food shops.

A boiled egg

The ultimate portable snack that ticks all the boxes in terms of convenience and durability is a hard-boiled-egg.

Simply pop a fresh egg into a pan of boiling water and let it cook for 10 minutes. Plunge into cold water to stop any black rings developing. If you are going to eat it straight away peel it under a running tap to ensure all of the shell is removed; if you are going to eat it later simply pop it into your pocket and peel when you are ready to eat. Best served with salt (one of those little packets you get in supermarket coffee shops is ideal).

Chapter 5

Hors d'oeuvres ......

Selwyn's

Extraordinarily Tasty
LAVERBREAD
Naturally Cooked Seaweed

SWANSEA BAY

SINCE 1948

The recipes in this chapter will get any dinner party guests talking – and they're all rich in B_{12}.

Laverbread hors d'oeuvre

Laverbread was introduced in 'Breakfasts' (page 27) as a rare plant source of vitamin B_{12}.

fresh or tinned laverbread
bacon fat

a little olive oil
salt and pepper

1   Fry as much laverbread as you require in a little bacon fat.

2   Add the olive oil after a minute's cooking.

3   Add salt and pepper to taste.

4   Serve spread on crackers, crispbread or fingers of toast.

Anchovies on toast

This is a really simple way to ensure you and your guests get a hit of B_{12} at your dinner party – anchovies have 11 mcg/100 g.

tinned anchovies (in strips) – how many you will need will depend on how many guests you are feeding, but you might want to allow four per person.

toasted bread – allow one slice for two people

butter

1   Toast the bread then cut off the side crusts. (Leave the crusts on the top and bottom as they help to stiffen the bread.)

2   Butter the toast, then cut it into really thin strips just a little wider than the anchovies, you should be able to get eight strips per slice of bread.

3   Place one anchovy fillet on each finger of toast – you may want to use a tweezers for this.

4   Serve to your guests.

Salami and cream cheese parcels

I'm going to assume that you don't want the hassle of making your own salami and as there are so many different types it would be difficult to choose just one, so use your own, or your guests' favourite. Salami generally contains 2 mcg/100 g B_{12} – the same as the cream cheese.

thinly sliced salami rounds   **cocktail sticks**
cream cheese

1   Carefully place something like a heaped teaspoon of the cheese in the centre of the salami disk. Fold up and secure with the cocktail stick.

2   Arrange on a plate and hand them around.

As an alternative to cream cheese, the tubed cheese on page 69 has an excellent amount of B_{12}.

Chapter 6

Dinner .....

Starters .....

Dinner has come to mean the main meal of the day but exactly what and when that is has changed over the centuries. In hot countries, the main meal of the day was always eaten in the evening when it was cooler, but in Western societies, dinner was usually eaten at midday, with the upper classes eating a supper at around 10 pm – after the theatre. Dinner gradually migrated to later in the day and by the 1850s, with the industrial revolution well under way, most working-class people would be eating their dinner after they had finished work at around 5 pm, although this was, and is, called 'tea' in many parts of the UK.

Let's just agree that for the purposes of this book, dinner is the main meal of the day which can either be formal, semi-formal or casual. It can consist of just one course or several. I've just concentrated on two courses, the starter and the main.

Avocados stuffed with crab

Serves four

100 g crabmeat – preferably fresh, but you can use canned
1 tsp Dijon mustard
2 tbsp olive oil
2 avocados

1 handful basil leaves (shredded with a few of the smaller leaves left whole, to serve)
chilli flakes to taste

1 Use a fork to fluff up the crabmeat.

2 Then add the mustard, oil, basil and chilli flakes and mix well.

3 Season to taste.

4 Cut the avocados in half and scoop out the stone.

5 Fill each avocado half with the crab mixture and serve.

Prawn cocktail

Serves four

This classic dish consists of prawns in a Marie Rose sauce. Although prawns don't have as much B_{12} as other seafoods, they still have a decent amount of the vitamin – grilled King Prawns have 2 mcg/100 g – and they are a firm favourite!

150 g pack cooked and peeled
  cold-water prawns
150 g pack cooked and peeled
  king prawns
1 tbsp chopped chives
½ iceberg lettuce, sliced
1 tbsp chopped chives
1 large avocado, stoned and diced
½ lemon, cut into wedges
½ a diced cucumber

For the Marie Rose sauce:

125 g mayonnaise
1 heaped tbsp tomato ketchup
¼ tsp tabasco sauce
½ lemon, juiced
½ tsp Worcestershire sauce

1   Begin by making the Marie Rose sauce – simply combine the ingredients together in a bowl and mix well before adding seasoning to taste.

2   Drain the prawns and place all of the cold-water prawns and half of the king prawns in a bowl and mix in half of the sauce and half of the chopped chives.

3   Add the lettuce to four glasses or shallow dishes. Some prefer half-pint beer glasses.

4   Add the juice of one quarter of the lemon to the avocado and add to the lettuce.

5   Then add the cucumber and the prawns mixed in the sauce.

6   Finish by adding the rest of the king prawns and sprinkle with the remaining chives.

Serve with the lemon wedges at the side.

If you want you can also add/provide some cayenne pepper or even some extra tobasco sauce.

Oysters

Oysters are a simple and, some would say, exotic start to a dinner. A 100gm serving gets you 324% of your daily intake of B_{12}. The only tricky bit is removing them from their shells (shucking). You'll need an oyster knife or a hefty screwdriver for this.

Allow three oysters per person – buy the freshest you can get hold of and make sure they are tightly closed

crushed ice or roughly ground sea salt
lemons, quartered (optional)
tobasco sauce (optional)

1   First, wash the oysters in cold water to remove any sand or grit. A stiff brush, such as a dedicated-to-the-kitchen nail brush, is ideal for this.

2   Place each oyster curved side down on a solid table, protecting your hand with a tea towel.

3   Locate the hinge that holds the bottom shell to the top shell and push the knife into the crack.

4   You want to prise the oyster open, which requires some effort.

5   When the oyster is open, discard the top shell.

6   There should be some seawater in the bottom shell around the oyster which you want to keep as that's the oyster liquor.

7   Carefully remove any bits of shell that may be on or around the oyster.

8   Arrange the salt or ice into a pile on a plate and then place the oyster, still in its shell, on top of the pile.

9   Serve with the lemon wedges and tobasco.

Simply swallow the oyster whole by tipping it into your mouth.

If you can't find any fresh oysters you can use tinned (smoked or unsmoked) that you can serve with crackers.

Mains.....

Steak and kidney pie

Serves six

This is a classic British pie that takes around 40 minutes to prepare – but the effort will be well worth it. The kidney is the main source of B_{12} in this recipe and the quantity can be increased for a richer pie if you prefer, but reduce the amount of the beef steak if you do so.

For the pastry:

250 g plain flour, plus a little
   extra for rolling
140 g cold unsalted butter,
   roughly cubed
1 large egg yolk

3 tbsp water
1 pinch sea salt (fine)
1 small egg, whisked with
1 tbsp milk, for the egg wash

First make the pastry:

1   Place the flour and salt into a food processor and blend for a few seconds.

2   Add the butter and blend to a consistency of rough breadcrumbs.

3   In a separate bowl, whisk the egg yolk with the water and then add to the food processor and blend until it all collects as a ball.

4   Remove from the food processor, wrap in cling-film and put it in the fridge for an hour or so.

5   If you don't have a food processor, use a large bowl and knead the ingredients together.

6   While the pastry is cooling, start on the filling.

(You can, of course, use ready-made pastry, either in a block or ready-rolled.
If you prefer a lid of puff pastry, you can use the ready-made products as used by chefs everywhere rather than making your own (it's a laborious task).

For the filling:

1 kg steak - any steak will do but you may prefer to use the cheaper cuts, such as braising or blade, as slow-cooking will make these tender.

400 g ox kidney - it has to be beef kidney as this is a slow-cook pie and pig or lamb's kidney will cook too quickly

50 g plain flour (you can add more if you prefer really thick gravy)

1 large onion

250 g flat mushrooms, unpeeled but wiped with a damp cloth

3 tbsp groundnut (peanut) or vegetable oil

100 g butter

2 splashes Worcestershire sauce (or more if you prefer)

600 ml fresh beef stock or 1 good quality stock cube in 600 ml boiling water'1 good quality beef stock

salt and pepper

bay leaf (optional)

1 egg, beaten for the pastry wash

For the filling:

1   Pre-heat the oven to 160°/fan 140°/gas 3. Cut the kidney into small slithers from around the white core – it really depends on you how big or small the slithers are but most people prefer small chunks. You can use a sharp knife or scissors. Dispose of the core.

2   Cut the beef into bite-sized cubes.

3   Slice the mushrooms.

4   Heat 1 tbsp of the oil in a large frying pan, toss in the kidney pieces and fry until lightly coloured. Transfer to a sieve or colander to drain.

5   Return the frying pan to the heat and add 25 g of the butter. When it is sizzling, add 1 tbsp of the oil.

6   Add the chopped onion and fry for around 8 minutes, stirring all the time until it's soft and light-brown.

7   Use a slotted spoon to remove the onion and kidneys from the oil and transfer to a large casserole dish.

8   Put 85 g flour into a large plastic bag, and add good pinches of salt and black pepper. Shake the flour and seasoning together and then add the chopped beef and shake until the meat is covered in flour.

9   Return the frying pan to a medium to high heat and add some more oil and butter if necessary.

10   Shake off any excess flour then fry the beef in batches until golden-brown. As each batch is done, transfer it to the casserole.

11   When all the beef is cooked and in the casserole, add a little more butter and oil and fry the mushrooms for about 2 minutes then add them to the casserole with the drained kidneys, hot water, stock cubes and bay leaf.

12   Add the left-over flour from the coating bag if you want a thick gravy.

13   Stir all the ingredients together, cover the casserole dish and place in the pre-heated oven.

14   Cook for about an hour and a half or until the meat is tender and the gravy to your liking.

15   After cooking, allow the mixture to cool thoroughly. This can take several hours. If you want, you can skim off any fat that has solidified during the cooling process though if left it will enhance the flavour.

Steak, kidney and oyster pie

This is an option that used to be popular when oysters were the food of the poor and were readily available and cheap.

To the steak and kidney pie filling, add a tin of smoked oysters that have been roughly chopped at the same time as you fry the onion.

Anglesey eggs

Serves four

This is an old Welsh dish that is said to have originated on the island of Anglesey off the north coast of Wales. The egg and cheese combination is a rich source of B_{12}

8 medium-sized eggs	1 kg mashing potatoes
1 large leek	2 tbsp milk
50 g butter, cut into 2 x 25 g pieces	black pepper to taste

1   First, boil the eggs for 10 minutes and then immediately plunge them into cold water (this stops them developing a black ring around the yolk).

2   When cool enough, peel the eggs under running water to make sure any shell is washed away. Halve or quarter them and set aside.

3   Trim and rinse the leek before dicing it finely.

4   Peel the potatoes and cut into even-sized chunks.

5   Then turn your oven on to pre-heat to 200°C/fan 180°C/gas 6.

6   Grease a baking dish with a little butter.

7   Heat 25 g butter in a frying pan and fry the leeks for about 5 minutes or until they are soft, then set aside.

8   Boil the potatoes in salted boiling water until they are mashable – about 15–20 minutes – drain them and add 25 g of butter and a little milk, but be careful not to add too much milk which will make the mix watery. Mash the potatoes (I use a hand whisk) until there are no lumps remaining, then add some salt and pepper to taste.

9   Tip in the cooked leeks and mix well.

10   Add the mixture to the baking dish and top with the boiled eggs.

Now for the sauce:

50 g butter
50 g plain flour
600 ml milk

150 g cheese, crumbled and
   separated into 2 portions
sea salt to taste

1   Add the flour and 25 g butter to a pan to make a roux, then gradually add the milk, stirring all the time until the sauce thickens.

2   Simmer the sauce for a few minutes before adding half of the cheese.

3   Cook for another minute, stirring all the time.

4   Pour the sauce over the mashed potatoes and eggs.

5   Sprinkle the remaining cheese over the dish (this will give a crisp topping).

6   Bake in the pre-heated oven for 15 to 20 minutes until the cheese has melted and the dish is bubbling.

This dish is suitable for vegetarians though it is traditionally served with hot or cold ham, which will give you even more vitamin B_{12}.

Lamb kebabs

Serves four

This is a recipe based on the Greek dish, souvlaki. The kebabs can be cooked on the barbecue, grill or griddle. At a push they can be cooked on a large frying pan. Ideally, the lamb should marinade in the fridge for two hours, but if you are in hurry you can skip that part.

60 ml olive oil
2 lemons, juiced
2 cloves garlic, crushed
1 tbsp dried oregano
1 good pinch of salt and black pepper

900 g diced lamb leg (If you can't get hold of ready diced lamb buy leg steaks and dice into small cubes)

8 wooden skewers

1   Set the skewers to soak in water to prevent them burning during cooking.

2   Mix the olive oil, lemon juice, garlic, oregano and the salt and pepper together in a suitable bowl.

3   Add the lamb cubes and stir vigorously to ensure all of the lamb is coated. If you have time, cover the bowl and marinate for 2 hours in the fridge.

4   Remove the kebab mixture from the fridge 15 minutes before cooking so that it reaches room temperature.

5   Carefully push the cubes onto the skewers. Each skewer should have the same number of cubes on it.

6   Ensure the barbecue/grill/griddle are hot before cooking the kebabs for 3-4 minutes each side. They should be charred on the outside and slightly pink on the inside. If you like your lamb well-cooked leave them for a little longer.

Serve with a Greek salad (mix together some lettuce, baby tomatoes, red onion and cucumber, and top with feta cheese, oregano, olive oil, lemon juice and black olives with salt and pepper to taste).

If you really want to go Greek make a tzatziki dip (grate some cucumber into Greek yoghurt, add some finely chopped mint and a crushed garlic clove and season to taste.

Steamed mussels on a bed of bladderwrack seaweed

Serves four

This is another fabulous recipe from the Pembrokeshire Beach Food Company. Bladderwrack seaweed was the original source of iodine and was used to treat goitre – a swelling of the thyroid gland caused by an iodine deficiency. You can of course leave the seaweed out if you can't get hold of any. The mermaids at the Pembrokeshire Beach Food Company like to cook this on the beach but it can be made just as easily in your kitchen.

2 kg mussels
bladderwrack – the amount will depend on how much you like the taste and on its availability
seawater to half cover the bladderwrack

2 lemons, quartered
fresh bread
Welsh Sea Black Butter

1   The first thing is to check your mussels; most shop-brought mussels have been prepared for you but it's always worth checking for dirt on the shell and that the beards have been pulled off.

2   Give your mussels a quick rinse in the sea/some water and put to one side.

3   Now it's time to put the pan on the fire, put your bladderwrack in it and then around an inch of seawater (enough so the bladderwrack is half covered).

4   Then add your lemons, squeezing some juice into the pan.

5   Cover the pan with tin foil and bring the seawater to the boil.

6   Once you have lots of steam coming out of the pan, put the mussels in the pan and cover again with tin foil.

7   Check the pan in approximately 5 minutes, and as soon as the mussels have opened, take the pan off the fire and dish up.

Serve with fresh baguettes and salted butter.

Lamb's liver and onion

Serves two

Most people's experience of eating liver would have been the leathery version served in school canteens, which would put you off eating liver for life. This is such a shame as cooked properly it really is a tasty dish that is high in B_{12} – a whopping 83 mcg/100 g.

15 g butter
1 onion, peeled and sliced
75 g smoked bacon lardons
1 garlic clove, peeled and crushed
1 medium
1 tbsp plain flour

salt and pepper
225 g lamb's liver, rinsed and sliced
1 tsp balsamic or red wine vinegar
300 ml boiling water
1 tbsp gravy granules

1   Heat the butter in a large frying pan.

2   Add the onion, bacon lardons and garlic.

3   Cook for 2-3 minutes.

4   Place the flour onto a plate and add the salt and pepper. Generously coat the liver with the flour.

5   Add the liver to the pan and brown for about 5 minutes.

6   Boil the water and add the gravy granules, giving it a good stir. Either serve the gravy separately or add it to the pan and coat the liver

Serve with mashed potatoes and seasonal vegetables.

Mussels in white wine

This makes a great starter or a light lunch as well as a main course. It is a little more refined than the beach version above. It can be made to sound more exotic by calling it 'Moules mariniere'. Cooked mussels have around 10 mcg/ 100 g.

1 kg mussels in their shells
large glass of white wine

1 finely chopped shallot
some parsley to garnish

1   Thoroughly rinse the mussels in a large bowl of water.

2   If any of the mussels have open shells, throw them away.

3   Pull off the beards of any mussels that have them. You may want to use a knife to help you. If any mussels are open, discard them as they are dead.

4   Rinse the mussels again and drain them before placing in a large pan along with the shallot and the wine. Don't overfill the pan as you are going to steam the mussels.

5   Cover the pan with a lid and put on a high heat.

6   Once the steaming begins, shake the pan and cook for a further 3 or 4 minutes. Shake a few more times.

7   Once the mussels have opened the cooking is complete.

8   Transfer the mussels to bowls, sprinkle them with the parsley and pour over the cooking liquor.

Enjoy with crusty bread.

Faggots and peas

Serves four (two faggots each)

This is a fabulous dish that is, thankfully, enjoying a revival. Faggots differ from meatballs in that they contain liver (which is the main source of the B_{12} in this dish). They are known as 'Ducks' or 'Savoury Ducks' in Lincolnshire, Yorkshire and Lancashire. In the Welsh mining village where I grew up there was an elderly butcher who was often to be seen standing in the doorway of his shop slowly eating one of his cold faggots, advertising to passers-by that his faggots were wholesome and contained only good quality ingredients. I often ask my local butcher for an 'open faggot' which is an individual faggot placed in a paper bag but left open so that I can enjoy it whilst walking to my office. You'll need a mincer to make these though you could use a food -processor but you will have to be careful not to allow the mixture to become a puree.

110 g pork shoulder
110 g pig's liver
250 g belly pork
any bacon scraps available
110 g breadcrumbs
1 onion, finely chopped

pinch mace
pinch allspice
2 sage leaves, finely chopped
salt and pepper to taste
streaky bacon (optional)

1   Pre-heat your oven to 190°C/fan 180°C/gas 5.

2   Roughly chop the pork shoulder, liver and belly pork then put in a mincer.

3   Once minced, transfer to a large mixing bowl and add all of the other ingredients. Mix well.

4   Using your washed and still wet hands, mould the mixture into eight balls (it's best to do this with wet hands).

5   If you want you can then wrap each individual faggot with the streaky bacon or caul (you'll have to ask you butcher for this). I prefer not to use anything.

6   Place the faggots onto a baking tray and bake in the pre-heated oven for about 50 minutes. You should get a nice browning on the top.

Serve immediately with peas and any gravy you might have.
Mashed potato or chips are a favourite accompaniment.

NB: If you don't have the time to prepare your own faggots, there are frozen ones available that are incredibly cheap and excellent value for money though they will contain a little more water than those that are homemade.

Bacon, cockle and Welshman's Caviar pie

Serves two

This is a recipe from the Pembrokeshire Beach Food Company (PBFC), who employ real mermaids to collect the shellfish and seaweed. This is as Welsh as it gets, and is a beautiful winter warmer. In this recipe we're using the PBFC's own toasted seaweed relish 'Welshman's Caviar'.

35 g butter (can use Welsh Sea Black Butter)
225 g smoked bacon
1/2 onion
35 g flour
1 egg

225 g cockles
2 tbsp Welshman's Caviar
single cream
puff pastry
pinch of white pepper

1   Pre-heat your oven to 185°C/180°C fan/gas 4.

2   Melt the butter in a pan and slowly cook the diced onion and bacon in it until slightly caramelised.

3   Add the flour and stir, cooking the flour through for a couple of minutes.

4   Slowly pour in the cream until you have a fairly thick, smooth sauce.

5   Add the Welshman's caviar and a pinch of white pepper as well as the cooked fresh cockles.

6   Place the mixture into an oven-proof dish and cut a puff pastry disk to place on top.

7   Brush with egg and cut a little hole in the pastry disc before placing the dish into the pre-heated oven.

8   Cook for around 25 minutes or until the pastry is golden and puffed.

Captain Cat's crab cakes

Serves two

Captain Cat is an old seafarer in Dylan Thomas's *Under Milk Wood.* This is another recipe from the Pembrokeshire Beach Food Company. It's the seasoning that makes this recipe stand out from other crab cakes. Captain Cat's Mor Seasoning can be bought online from the Pembrokeshire Beach Food Company's website. *Mor* is Welsh for sea.

250 g mixed crab meat (50/50 brown/ white)
6 Ship's Biscuits, crumbled
1 tbsp mayo
$^1/_2$ tsp Dijon mustard

$^1/_4$ tsp Worcestershire sauce
1 egg
$^1/_2$ tsp Captain Cat's *Mor* Seasoning
handful of dry breadcrumbs

1   Mix together all of the ingredients apart from the breadcrumbs.

2   Sprinkle the breadcrumbs onto a plate.

3   Shape the crab mix into patties of the desired size and coat with breadcrumbs.

4   Shallow-fry until golden brown.

Serve with lemon and mayo.

Spaghetti vongole

Serves four

One of the highest concentrations of B$_{12}$ is to be found in clams, which can be bought in high-end fishmongers or fish markets. There are several types of clams and any will do. If you really cannot source any then use mussels or cockles, but they must be fresh and not in vinegar.

500 g small clams
350 g spaghetti
30 g butter
2 tbsp olive oil
3 cloves garlic, finely chopped or
    pressed

chilli, finely chopped (strength and
    quantity according to taste)
100 ml dry white wine
flat-leaf parsley, roughly chopped
tsp lemon juice

1   Rinse the clams in cold running water, and scrub if necessary, then put them into a large bowl of cold water so that all of them are covered. Add plenty of salt and leave for a couple of hours, then drain and rinse once again to ensure there is no grit or sand in them and then drain them.

2   Put the spaghetti into a large pan of salted boiling water and cook for a couple of minutes under the recommended time, until nearly done.

3   Put half the butter and the olive oil in a large pan over a medium heat and soften the garlic and chilli.

4   Add the clams, and turn up the heat. Pour in the wine, cover and leave for a couple of minutes until most of them have opened. Throw away any that remain closed. Add the others to the sauce still in their shells.

5   Some people pick a few from their shells to make the dish a little more interesting.

6   Drain the spaghetti and add to the pan along with the remaining butter.

7   Toss well and leave for a minute, then stir through the chopped parsley and lemon juice.

Add salt and pepper to taste and serve.

Chapter 7

Desserts .....

There are no desserts that are rich in B$_{12}$, though there are some foods that can add a little to your daily intake.

- Homemade custard made with semi-skimmed milk contains 0.9 mcg/100 g.
- This is the same as homemade rice pudding. Though ready-to-eat custard contains just 0.2 mcg/100 g and tinned rice pudding contains just a small 'trace' of the vitamin, meaning there's some B$_{12}$ in it but not enough to measure.
- You could have a soft-scoop ice-cream that offers 0.5 mcg/100 g whilst a 'cornetto-style' version yields 0.7 mcg/100 g.
- A 100 g portion of tiramisu has 0.4 mcg of B$_{12}$ in it.

Chapter 8

Other sources .....

In recent years there has been an increase in the development and supply of various types of supplements that contain large amounts of B_{12}. These include tablets and lozenges, sub-lingual sprays (one spray of the leading brand gets you 12,000% of your daily requirement), ointments, skin-patches and nasal sprays. Injections of B_{12} can be bought at many beauty parlours and even hairdressers.

There are also a growing number of nutritional supplements that offer substantial amounts of B_{12}, including soft drinks, powders that can be added to drinks or food and even seaweed preparations. Some of these are aimed at the increasing number of people who have rejected animal products as food and become either vegetarians or vegans.

There is some discussion as to whether these forms of B_{12} contain 'genuine' B_{12}, or whether they offer only 'analogues' of B_{12}. This is a discussion that I don't want to get involved in as the science is really very complex. However, it's interesting that so many businesses have realised that there is a need for people, whether they be vegetarian, vegan or not, to consume adequate amounts of B_{12} and are manufacturing products that allow them these benefits.

As for drinks and B_{12}, well hot beverages made with beef extract such as Bovril or or from stock cubes such as Oxo (sometimes known as 'beef tea') contain decent amounts of B_{12} though how much will depend on how diluted the drink is.

Then there's another interesting source of B_{12} and one that is growing in popularity - insects: 'Vitamin B_{12} is found in abundance in larvae of the yellow mealworm beetle *T. molitor* (0.47 mcg per 100 g) and the house cricket *Acheta domesticus* (5.4 mcg per 100 g in adults, 8.7 mcg per 100 g in nymphs). However, many other species that have been analysed contain only negligible amounts of this vitamin'.

Appendix I
Sources of B$_{12}$ in foods

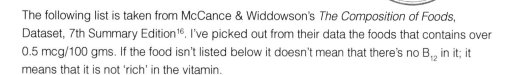

The following list is taken from McCance & Widdowson's *The Composition of Foods*, Dataset, 7th Summary Edition[16]. I've picked out from their data the foods that contains over 0.5 mcg/100 gms. If the food isn't listed below it doesn't mean that there's no B$_{12}$ in it; it means that it is not 'rich' in the vitamin.

'Fortified' means that a form of B$_{12}$ has been added.
'Trace' (Tr) means there is some B$_{12}$ but too little to measure accurately.

Cereals   mcg/100 g

Egg fried rice. . . . . Tr
Macaroni cheese. 0.7
Egg pasta . . . . Tr
Ravioli, meat, canned . . . . Tr
Croissants . . . . Tr
Cheese and pickle sandwich 0.7

Breakfast cereals

Bran Flakes (fortified) 2.3
Corn Flakes (fortified) 1.9
Corn Flakes, unfortified . . . . Tr
Malted wheat flakes. 3.4
Malted wheat cereal 1.9
Chocolate-flavoured rice. 1.9
Wheat biscuits. 0.0
Shredded wheat-style 0.0

Biscuits and cakes – just very small or trace amounts

Homemade sponge cakes 0.9

Pastry – just very small or 'trace'

Chocolate eclairs. 0.3
Scones homemade 0.4

Savouries

Cheese and onion pastry roll 0.5
Pancakes, savoury semi-skimmed 1.0
Yorkshire pudding 1.0

Pizza – very little or trace

Fish topped 1.0
Meat topped 0.8

Milk and milk products

Whole pasteurised. . . . . 0.9 average
Semi-skimmed pasteurised. . . . . 0.9 average
UHT. 0.2
Sheep's milk 0.6
Soya milk. 0.4
Double cream 0.6
Clotted cream 0.1

Cheeses – all cheeses have some B$_{12}$ even processed ones

Cheddar 2.4
Cheese spread (red fat) 2.0
Cottage cheese. . . . . 0.6 (full-fat or reduced)
Edam. 2.1
Parmesan, fresh 3.3

Yoghurts and fromage frais

Fromage frais, fat-free. 1.4
Yoghurt plain 0.2
Yoghurt whole milk 0.3

Ice creams

Cornetto-type 0.7
Soft-scoop vanilla 0.5

Puddings and chilled desserts – very little or trace in pies and
crumbles incl. Christmas pudding

Cheesecake – fruit filled frozen. 0.5
Custard – semi-skimmed. 0.9
Custard, ready-to-eat 0.2
Rice pudding, canned. . . . . Tr
Rice pudding, homemade. 0.9
Fruit trifle 0.2
Tiramisu. 0.4

Eggs and egg dishes

Chicken eggs, raw 2.7
Chicken eggs, boiled 2.0
Poached 1.8

Fried in sunflower oil 1.0
Scrambled with semi-skimmed milk 2.4
Plain omelette 2.3
Cheese omelette 2.3
Cheese and egg quiche 1.5
Quiche Lorraine S/C pastry. 0.5

Fats and oils

Butter, salted 0.3
Butter, spreadable. 0.1
Fat-spread, polyunsaturated. . . . . Tr
Suet, olive oil etc 0.0
Lard . . . . Tr

Meat and meat products

Back bacon, grilled 1.0
Gammon, boiled . . . . Tr
Beef fat 1.0
Braising steak 3.0
Rump steak, barbecued 3.0
Topside, roasted 2.0
Veal escalope, fried. 4.0
Lamb leg, roasted 2.0
Lamb chops, grilled 3.0
Lamb kebabs 3.0
Pork leg 1.0
Pork chops 1.0
Chicken breast, grilled . . . . Tr
Chicken drumsticks. . . . . Tr
Chicken whole. . . . . Tr
Turkey dark meat. 2.0
Turkey light meat 1.0
Turkey thighs, casseroled 2.0
Duck, crispy Chinese-style 3.0
Duck roasted. 3.0
Goose, roasted 2.0
Pheasant 3.0
Rabbit, stewed . . . . 3.0 (raw, it's 10.0)
Venison 1.0

Offal

Lamb's heart 06.0
Lamb's kidneys 54.0
Ox kidney 38.0
Calf's liver, fried 45.00

Lamb's liver, fried. 83.00
Ox's liver, stewed. 110.00

Beefburgers

98–99% beef, grilled 3.0
62-85% beef, grilled 2.0
98-99% beef, fried. 3.0
Cheeseburger 2.0

Other

Steak and kidney pie. 4.0
Black pudding. 1.0
Chicken breast/steak coated 3.0
Chicken pieces, coated T/A 2.0
Chicken portions, battered D/Fry . . . . Tr
Corned beef 2.0
Cornish pasty . . . . Tr
Frankfurter 1.0
Haggis, boiled. 2.0
Liver sausage 10.0
Meat spread 3.0
Paté, liver. 8.0
Paté, liver – reduced fat 12.0
Pork pie . . . . Tr
Salami 2.0
Sausages, beef, grilled 1.0
Pork sausage, full and reduced fat 1.0
Pork sausage, premium 1.0
Sausage roll. . . . . Tr
Scotch egg 1.0
Steak and kidney pie, homemade. 4.0
Beef stew, homemade. 1.0
Beef bourguignon 1.0
Beef Bolognese sauce 1.0
Chicken chow mein. . . . . Tr
Chicken fajita. . . . . Tr
Chicken tandoori. 1.0
Chicken wings. 1.0
Cottage/shepherd's pie. 1.0
Doner kebab 2.0
Faggots in gravy 6.0
Irish stew 1.0
Lasagne. 1.0
Moussaka 1.0
Pork spare ribs 1.0

Shish kebab, meat only 3.0
Spaghetti Bolognese . . . . N

White fish

Cod, baked 2.0
Cod, battered, baked 2.0
Battered take-away 2.0
Coley, baked 3.0
Haddock 2.0
Lemon sole 1.0
Plaice 2.0
Pollock, baked 4.0
Sea bass, baked 3.0

Fatty fish

Anchovies, canned 11.0
Herring, grilled 15.0
Kippers 11.0
Mackerel, grilled 9.0
Mackerel, smoked 10.0
Salmon, grilled, farmed 3.0
Salmon, hot-smoked 4.0
Salmon, cold-smoked 3.0
Salmon, pink, canned 5.0
Salmon, red, canned 5.0
Sardines, grilled 11.0
Sardines, canned in brine 11.0
Sardines, canned in tomato sauce 9.0
Sardines, canned in olive oil 15.0
Sardines, canned in sunflower oil 15.0
Rainbow trout, baked 3.0
Tuna canned in brine or SF 3.0

Crustacea

Crab, cooked 13.0
Prawns, king, grilled 2.0
Scampi, in breadcrumbs and baked 2.0
Scampi, in breadcrumbs fried 1.0

Molluscs

Calamari, batter-baked 2.0
Cockles, boiled 47.0
Mussels in white wine 9.0

Fish products

Prawn curry takeaway	Tr
Fishcakes B/C baked	1.0
Fishfingers, cod, grilled/baked	2.0
Fish pie, homemade	1.0
Kedgeree, homemade	2.0
Seafood selection	15.0
Seafood sticks	1.0
Sushi, salmon nigiri	1.0
Taramasalata	3.0
Tuna paté	3.0

Vegetable dishes

Cauliflower cheese made with semi-skimmed milk	0.50

Sugars, preserves and snacks

Milk chocolate	2.1
Plain chocolate	0.0
Crème egg	1.0
Maltesers and similar	1.3

Beverages

Build-up shake power	2.3	made with milk
Horlicks. powder	1.2	made with milk
Ovaltine	2.5	made with milk

Alcohol

Most alcoholic drinks include only a trace.

Soups, sauces and miscellaneous foods

Oxtail	Tr
Cheese sauce, homemade	1.1
(Cheese sauce, dried packet mix	0.0)
White sauce	0.9

Chutney, dips, piccalilli – most are 0 or Tr, and the same for salad dressings other than:

Salad cream	0.5
Mayonnaise	0.3
reduced-fat	0.5
Yeast extract, fortified	15.0

Nothing in: curry paste, pesto, mint sauce, soy sauce, sweet and sour, tomato ketchup or Worcestershire sauce, pasta sauce, curry sauces.

Appendix II
'Diet in the anemias'

As I mentioned earlier on in the book page 11, patients with pernicious anaemia used to die due to their inability to absorb vitamin B_{12} from food. Then, during the 1920s, serendipity led to patients being kept alive by eating raw, or partially cooked, liver. A booklet by the pharmaceutical company Eli Lilly and Company entitled *The Anemias*, published in 1938, has a section that contains various recipes that it was hoped would help the patient to live. At the time of publication B_{12} hadn't been 'discovered'. I have been unable to find out just how successful these recipes were in keeping patients with pernicious anaemia alive; presumably this approach wasn't ideal as injections were soon developed, first as liver injections and then later B_{12}.

Here is a selection of recipes from the little booklet, **but please do not use these recipes to treat your pernicious anaemia.**

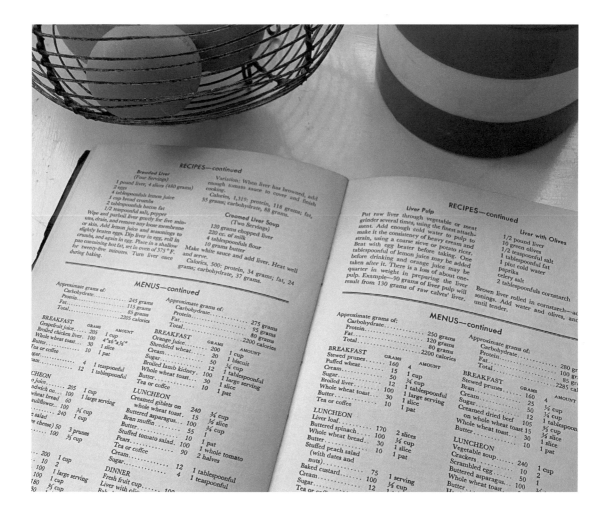

General remarks

The patient was instructed to provide himself (sic) with the following foods in the amounts indicated daily:

At least 160 to 240 g (¹/₃ to ½ lb) cooked weight of calves' or beef liver daily, cooked as little as possible

At least 120 g (¹/₄ lb) red muscle-meat cooked rare.

5 oz grape juice (142 g)

It also provided some useful recipes that you are welcome to try in order to ensure that there is no deficiency of B_{12} in your diet.

Liver drink

2 oz liver (60 g)   5 oz grape juice (142 g)

1 Sieve the liver through a coarse strainer.

2 Beat the pulp and juice with a Dover egg beater until the liver is thoroughly mixed. Tomato or orange juice may be substituted for the grape juice.
   The grape juice seems to disguise the liver taste better than the other juices.

And after that little aperitif we go to the first course – soup:

Creamed liver soup

two servings

120 g chopped liver   4 tbsp flour
220 cc milk   10 g butter

1   Make a white sauce and add the liver.

2   Heat well and serve.

Day menu for pernicious anaemia patients

Here's a typical day's menu for patients.

Food	Grams	Amount

Breakfast

Food	Grams	Amount
Stewed prunes	160	4
Puffed wheat	15	1 cup
Cream	50	¼ cup
Sugar	12	1 tbsp
Broiled liver	100	1 large serving
Whole wheat toast	30	1 slice
Butter	10	1 pat
Tea or coffee		

Lunch

Food	Grams	Amount
Liver loaf	70	2 slices
On other days patients were offered		
Creamed giblets on whole wheat toast	240	¾ cup
Liver sandwich	100	1 large serving
Buttered spinach	100	¾ cup
Whole-wheat bread	30	1 slice
Butter	10	1 pat
Stuffed peach salad (with dates and nuts)	75	1 serving
Baked custard	100	½ cup
Cream	12	1 tbp
Sugar	4	1 tsp
Tea or coffee		

Dinner

Food	Grams	Amount
Vegetable soup	255	1 cup
With ground liver	30	2 tbsp
Broiled steak	110	6"x41/2x3/4
With mushrooms	25	¼ cup
Buttered beets	100	¾ cup
Cabbage slaw	100	1 cup
Whole wheat bread	30	1 slice
Butter	10	1 pat

Tea or coffee

Cream . . . . .12. . . . . 1 tbsp

Sugar. . . . . .4. . . . . 1 tsp

Pineapple (fresh or canned) . . . . .100 . . . . 2 slices

References

Foreword

1. Miller JW. Proton Pump Inhibitors, H2-Receptor Antagonists, Metformin, and Vitamin B-12 Deficiency: Clinical Implications. *Adv Nutr* 2018; *9*: 511S-518S.

2. Smith AD, et al. Vitamin B12. *Adv Food Nutr Res* 2018; *83*: 215-279.

Introduction

3. Mikkelsen K, Apostolopoulos V. (2019) Vitamin B12, Folic Acid, and the Immune System. In: Mahmoudi M, Rezaei N (eds). *Nutrition and Immunity*. Springer,

4. Vitamin B12 – best sources for vegans and vegetarians. *ATP Science* 7 October 2016. https://atpscience.co.uk/the-best-sources-of-vitamin-b12-for-veganvegetarians/ (Accessed 15 March 2020.)

5. Watanabe F, Bito T. Vitamin B12 sources and microbial interaction. *Exp Biol Med* 2018; 243(2): 148–158. doi:10.1177/1535370217746612

6. Devalia V, Hamilton MS, Molloy A-M. Guidelines for the diagnosis and treatment of cobalamin and folate disorders. *British Journal of Haematology* 2014; 166(4): 496-513.

7. Duckett J. Mintel Report: Vitamins and Supplements. UK - Sept 2016. *Mintel Reports* https://reports.mintel.com/display/748735/#

8. HFMA. Industry Facts. www.hfma.co.uk/media-events/industry-facts/ (Accessed 27 Nov 2019.)

Breakfasts

9. Guarino B. Scientists Have Discovered The Earliest Evidence of Bread, And It's Much Older Than We Expected. *The Washington Post* 17th July 2018.

10. Anderson HA. *Breakfast: A History.* AltaMira Press, 2013.

11. Watanabe F, Yabuta Y, Bito T, Teng F. Vitamin B_{12}-containing plant food sources for vegetarians. *Nutrients* 2014; 6(5): 1861–1873. doi:10.3390/nu6051861

12. 50 per cent of Britons now don't have time for breakfast according to new survey. *Daily Express* 16 January 2017. www.express.co.uk/life-style/food/754711/Breakfast-skipping-Britain-meal-health (accessed 8 May 2020)

Lunch

13. Beeton I. *The Book of Household Management*. Farrar, Straus, and Giroux. 1861: pp 959.

14. Marks K. BLT: British, lousy and tasteless. *The Independent*,. London, UK. 17 May 1997. www.independent.co.uk/news/blt-british-lousy-and-tasteless-1261881.html (accessed 8 May 2020)

Other sources

15. Kou imská L, Adámková A. Nutritional and sensory quality of edible insects. *NFS Journal* 2016; 4: 22–26.

Appendix 1

16. Finglas PM, Roe MA, Pinchen MA, Berry R, Church SM, Dodhia SK, Farron-Wilson M, Swan G. *McCance and Widdowson's The Composition of Foods*, 7th Summary Edition. Royal Society of Chemistry; Cambridge, UK.

Index

Also by Martyn Hooper...

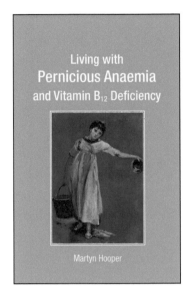

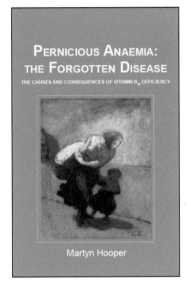

Pernicious Anaemia: The Forgotten Disease

Find out about the importance of B_{12}, the consequences of deficiency and the problems of diagnosing and treating pernicious anaemia

Living with Pernicious Anaemia and Vitamin B_{12} Deficiency

How can if be that despite regular B_{12} injections, you can continue to have all the symptoms of deficiency? Martyn Hooper talks through the challenges of everyday life based on the experience of members of the Pernicious Anaemia Society

What You Need to Know About Pernicious Anaemia and Vitamin B_{12} Deficiency

'Every doctor should read this book.'
Dr Chris Steele MBE

'A "must read" for patients and doctors alike.'
Lyn Mynott, Chair.Chief Executive, Thyroid UK